DINOSAURS

INCREDIBLE BUT TRUE FACTS

This edition published by Parragon Books Ltd in 2016
and distributed by

Parragon Inc.
440 Park Avenue South, 13th Floor
New York, NY 10016
www.parragon.com

English translation edited by Robyn Newton
and Nicola Barber
Consultants: John Cooper and Michael J. Benton
Translated by Elena Horas

ISBN 978-1-4748-5035-3

Printed in China

DINOSAURS

INCREDIBLE BUT TRUE FACTS

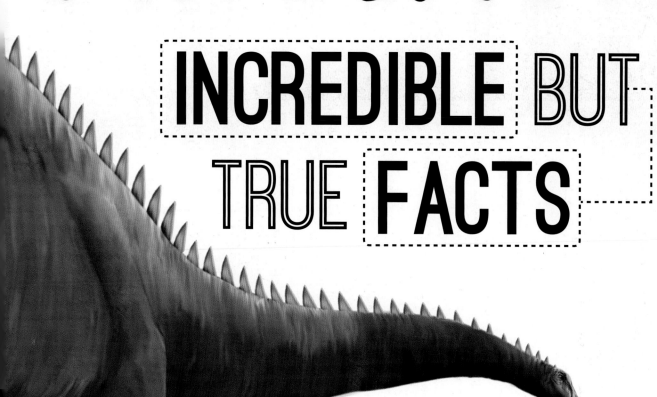

PaRragon

Bath · New York · Cologne · Melbourne · Delhi
Hong Kong · Shenzhen · Singapore

CONTENTS

Introduction

Ever since the first dinosaur bones were brought to light nearly two hundred years ago, people have been fascinated by these extinct creatures. The term *dinosaur* comes from two Greek words meaning "terrible lizard." It was first used in 1842 by the British paleontologist Sir Richard Owen. Paleontologists study fossils and other evidence of ancient life to learn about the history of our planet. Every fossil is a clue, and from these clues they can build up a picture of life in prehistoric times.

Our planet was formed around 4.6 billion years ago. The first living creatures appeared roughly 1.2 billion years later. These organisms developed from single-celled to multicelled organisms, and they gradually moved from rivers and oceans onto dry land.

The dinosaurs existed during a period of time known as the Mesozoic era. At first, they lived on the Pangaea supercontinent, the only landmass on the planet at that time. Gradually their population increased, and they became extremely varied, until they were the most common form of life on land. Enormous herbivores (plant-eaters) such as *Diplodocus* roamed the land alongside powerful predators such as *Giganotosaurus*. But by the end of the Mesozoic era, 65 million years ago, there were no dinosaurs left on Earth.

Scientists still debate what could have happened to cause this mass extinction.

For a long time, many paleontologists thought that all dinosaurs were slow-moving creatures, with behavior similar to some reptiles of today. But more recent evidence has suggested that many of the dinosaurs were fast, active creatures that probably lived in groups and traveled long distances. Skin impressions from dinosaurs have also revealed that some of them had feathers. This great discovery was one of the clues that helped to link the dinosaurs to birds.

The study of dinosaurs continues to attract the interest of experts and the public alike. Whatever advances are made in the field of paleontology, there are always many questions that remain to be answered, and there is always something new to find!

BEFORE
THE DINOSAURS

Life on planet Earth started
in the seas and oceans.
Creatures appeared in great
numbers and amazing forms.
As they evolved and adapted
to their surroundings,
life forms gradually began
to appear on land as well.

Beginning of Life

Scientists divide time into eras in order to talk about events that have happened throughout history and help understand life on Earth. Eras are then divided into periods, epochs, and ages to describe shorter amounts of time.

PRECAMBRIAN ERA

The Precambrian era spanned more than 4 billion years. Its beginning marked the point when the solid crust of the Earth began to develop from liquid rock, known as lava. Then, around 2.1 billion years ago, oxygen started to form in the atmosphere.

PALEOZOIC ERA

The Paleozoic era started with an explosion of life in Earth's oceans. It ended with the biggest destruction of species in Earth's history, when nearly 90 percent of sea life perished. During this era, reptiles, amphibians, and insects developed on land.

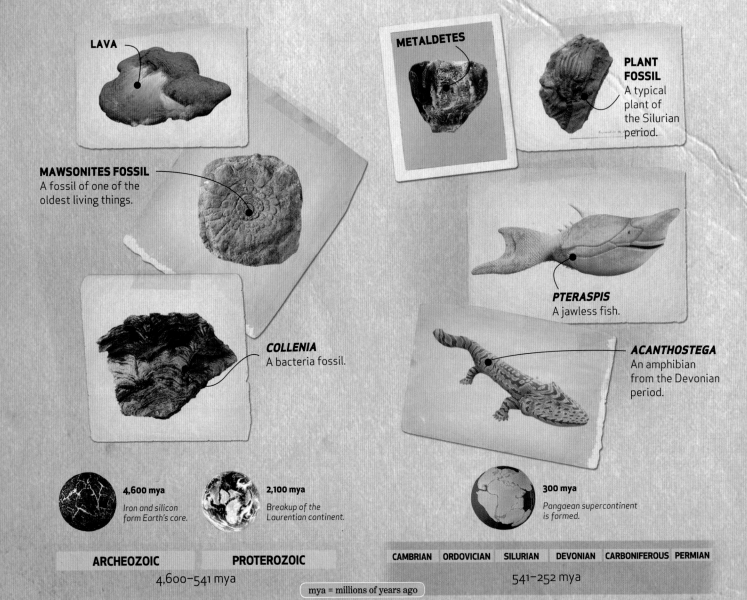

LAVA

METALDETES

PLANT FOSSIL
A typical plant of the Silurian period.

MAWSONITES FOSSIL
A fossil of one of the oldest living things.

COLLENIA
A bacteria fossil.

PTERASPIS
A jawless fish.

ACANTHOSTEGA
An amphibian from the Devonian period.

4,600 mya
Iron and silicon form Earth's core.

2,100 mya
Breakup of the Laurentian continent.

300 mya
Pangaean supercontinent is formed.

ARCHEOZOIC	PROTEROZOIC		CAMBRIAN	ORDOVICIAN	SILURIAN	DEVONIAN	CARBONIFEROUS	PERMIAN

4,600–541 mya

541–252 mya

mya = millions of years ago

4,600 mya Formation of Earth	3,400 mya First bacteria (single-celled organisms) appear	2,100 mya Oxygen forms in the atmosphere	700 mya First multicellular animals appear

PRECAMBRIAN

PALEOZOIC

MESOZOIC

CENOZOIC

TIMELINE

For the greatest part of history, organisms with only one cell were the main life forms on Earth. The first organisms made up of many cells (multicellular) appeared 700 million years ago.

MESOZOIC ERA

The Mesozoic era was the time of the dinosaurs. Other reptiles included tortoises, crocodiles, lizards, and snakes. Birds, mammals, and the first flowering plants also appeared. The era ended with the disappearance of many life forms.

CENOZOIC ERA

The dawn of the Cenozoic era saw the extinction of the dinosaurs. Since then, mammals have dominated, and birds have increased in number. At this most recent time in Earth's long history, human beings appeared.

GIGANOTOSAURUS

BAROSAURUS
Huge herbivore (plant-eater) that lived 150 million years ago.

BAROSAURUS
BONE

TITANIS
One of the first birds.

THYLACOSMILUS
A saber-toothed marsupial.

AUSTRALOPITHECUS
A human ancestor.

200–180 mya
Breakup of Pangaea into continents. Africa, India, and America separate.

60 mya
Continents are already similar to present-day landmasses, and mountains are being formed.

TRIASSIC	JURASSIC	CRETACEOUS

252–66 mya

TERTIARY	QUATERNARY

From 66 mya to present times

SPECIES
OF DINOSAURS

At the end of the Triassic period, the dinosaurs took over from the reptiles that dominated our planet previously. They developed into many different shapes and sizes and ruled Earth.

What Is a Dinosaur?

Dinosaurs were reptiles that appeared about 230 million years ago. They evolved into an amazing variety of shapes and types: some were giants, others small; some herbivores, others carnivores. They had horns, crests, bony plates, and even feathers as protection. The dinosaurs disappeared in the Cretaceous period but left behind descendants that could fly and had feathers—birds!

D inosaurs looked different from tortoises, lizards, and crocodiles because of their body posture. Their limbs came downward from their bodies, not out from their sides, as in most reptiles. Their posture was straighter, and they were able to move faster and more gracefully than other reptiles. Dinosaurs could rise onto their rear legs and use their toes when walking or running. This more efficient way of moving was one of the keys to the dinosaurs' success against the competition of other reptilian species.

Many dinosaur species reached gigantic sizes. *Argentinosaurus* and *Puertasaurus* are considered the largest land animals ever. They reached almost 115 feet from the tip of the nose to the end of the tail. But not all dinosaurs were huge. There were some dinosaurs the same size as chickens, such as *Scipionyx* from Italy, *Microraptor* from China, and *Ligabueino* from Argentina.

TAIL
A long and robust tail was used to balance the weight of the body.

NECK
This part of the body became S-shaped.

LEGS
The structure of the legs and hips was similar to that of present-day birds.

THE EVOLUTION OF REPTILES

As dinosaurs evolved from reptiles, the main changes were related to movement, from reptilian to bipedal (two-footed) forms.

1 REPTILIAN

In lizards, the limbs spread outward, with elbows and knees bending, and the belly dragging on the ground.

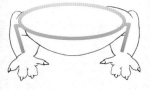

2 SEMIERECT

In crocodiles, the limbs stretch outward and downward, with elbows and knees bent at an angle of 45 degrees. Crocodiles crawl when moving slowly and straighten their legs when running.

3 BIPEDS

In dinosaurs, the rear limbs were straight beneath the body, so that the body was never dragged, not even when the dinosaur was walking very slowly.

Classification

This chart shows the relationships among the groups of dinosaurs, starting from the main divisions (Saurischia and Ornithischia) when they first evolved from early reptiles in the Triassic period. Over the next 160 million years they evolved into many different groups.

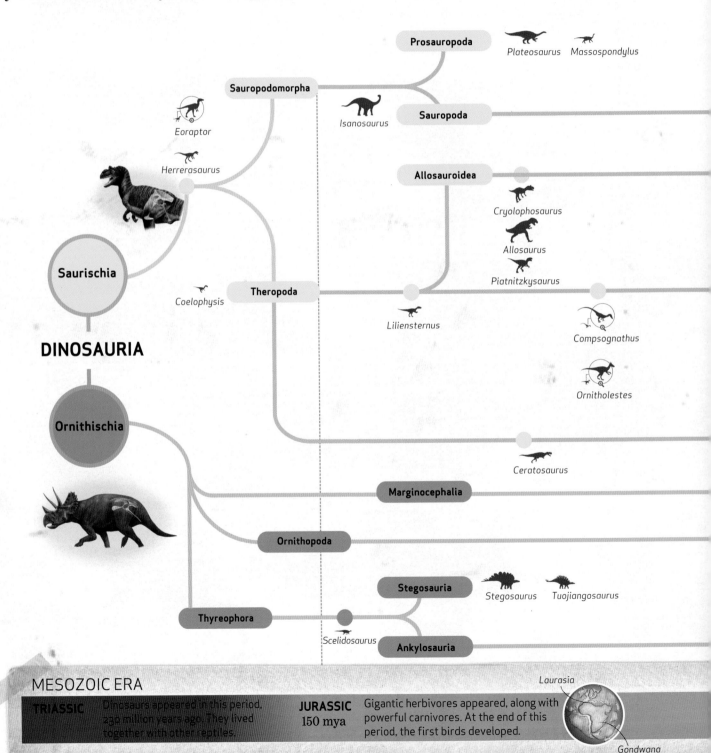

Prosauropoda — Plateosaurus, Massospondylus

Sauropodomorpha

Eoraptor

Herrerasaurus

Isanosaurus — **Sauropoda**

Saurischia

Allosauroidea

Cryolophosaurus

Allosaurus

Piatnitzkysaurus

DINOSAURIA

Coelophysis — **Theropoda**

Liliensternus

Compsognathus

Ornitholestes

Ornithischia

Ceratosaurus

Marginocephalia

Ornithopoda

Stegosauria — Stegosaurus, Tuojiangosaurus

Thyreophora

Scelidosaurus

Ankylosauria

MESOZOIC ERA

TRIASSIC Dinosaurs appeared in this period, 230 million years ago. They lived together with other reptiles.

JURASSIC 150 mya Gigantic herbivores appeared, along with powerful carnivores. At the end of this period, the first birds developed.

Laurasia

Gondwana

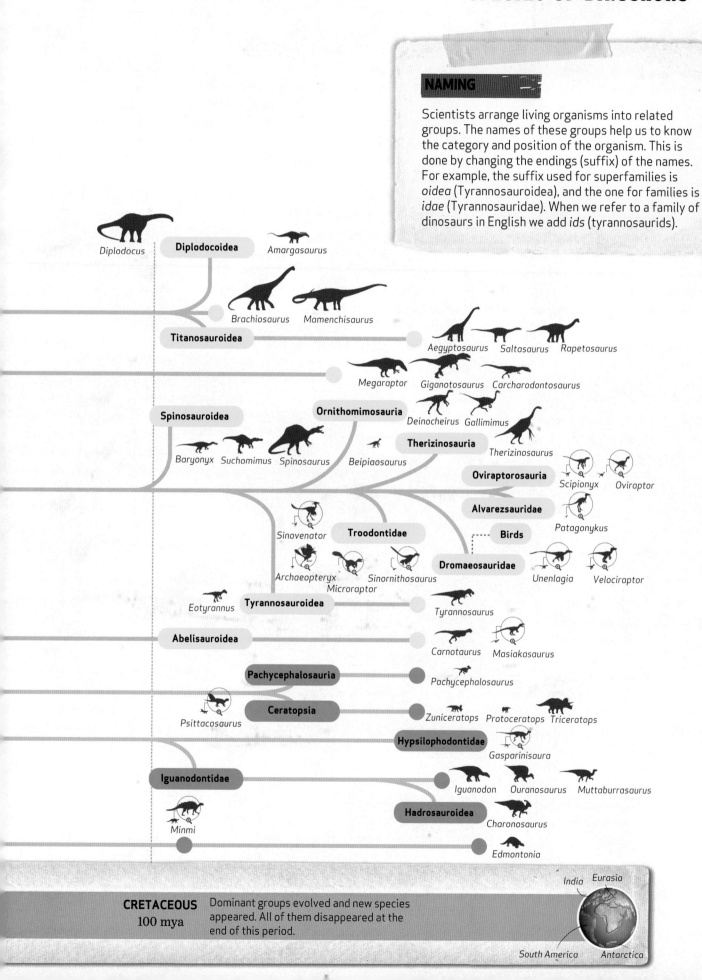

NAMING

Scientists arrange living organisms into related groups. The names of these groups help us to know the category and position of the organism. This is done by changing the endings (suffix) of the names. For example, the suffix used for superfamilies is *oidea* (Tyrannosauroidea), and the one for families is *idae* (Tyrannosauridae). When we refer to a family of dinosaurs in English we add *ids* (tyrannosaurids).

Diplodocus

Diplodocoidea

Amargasaurus

Brachiosaurus

Mamenchisaurus

Titanosauroidea

Aegyptosaurus   Saltasaurus   Rapetosaurus

Megaraptor   Giganotosaurus   Carcharodontosaurus

Spinosauroidea

Ornithomimosauria

Deinocheirus   Gallimimus

Baryonyx   Suchomimus   Spinosaurus

Beipiaosaurus

Therizinosauria

Therizinosaurus

Oviraptorosauria

Scipionyx   Oviraptor

Alvarezsauridae

Patagonykus

Troodontidae

Birds

Sinovenator

Dromaeosauridae

Archaeopteryx   Sinornithosaurus

Microraptor

Unenlagia   Velociraptor

Eotyrannus

Tyrannosauroidea

Tyrannosaurus

Abelisauroidea

Carnotaurus   Masiakasaurus

Pachycephalosauria

Pachycephalosaurus

Psittacosaurus

Ceratopsia

Zuniceratops   Protoceratops   Triceratops

Hypsilophodontidae

Gasparinisaura

Iguanodontidae

Iguanodon   Ouranosaurus   Muttaburrasaurus

Minmi

Hadrosauroidea

Charonosaurus

Edmontonia

CRETACEOUS
100 mya

Dominant groups evolved and new species appeared. All of them disappeared at the end of this period.

India   Eurasia

South America   Antarctica

Tyrannosaurus rex

Tyrannosaurus rex had a huge head, strong and sharp teeth, and legs well suited for running. This dinosaur was one of the most extraordinary creatures of the prehistoric world!

Tyrannosaurus rex and its close relatives, the tyrannosaurids, evolved in the Northern Hemisphere in the late Cretaceous period. Skeletons, teeth, and footprints of these carnivores have been found in North America and Central Asia.

They were great hunters. Their favorite prey included ceratopsians and hadrosaurs. The larger tyrannosaurids lived alongside the dromaeosaurids (small-sized, fast-running carnivorous dinosaurs).

The strength of *Tyrannosaurus* lay in its huge jaws, powered by muscles in its temples. The shape of the skull hints that it had a good sense of smell, which helped it to find prey.

There have been many different theories about the feeding habits of *Tyrannosaurus*. It was once thought that it was unable to hunt successfully! But this may not be true. Its hind legs show that it would have been able to pick up enough speed to hunt heavy animals that could not run as fast. Skeletons of *Triceratops* and other hadrosaurs have been found with large teeth marks, thought to have been made by tyrannosaurids. This clue leads us to believe that *Tyrannosaurus* would have been able to capture its prey alive. However, during long periods of drought, it was likely to have scavenged for leftovers.

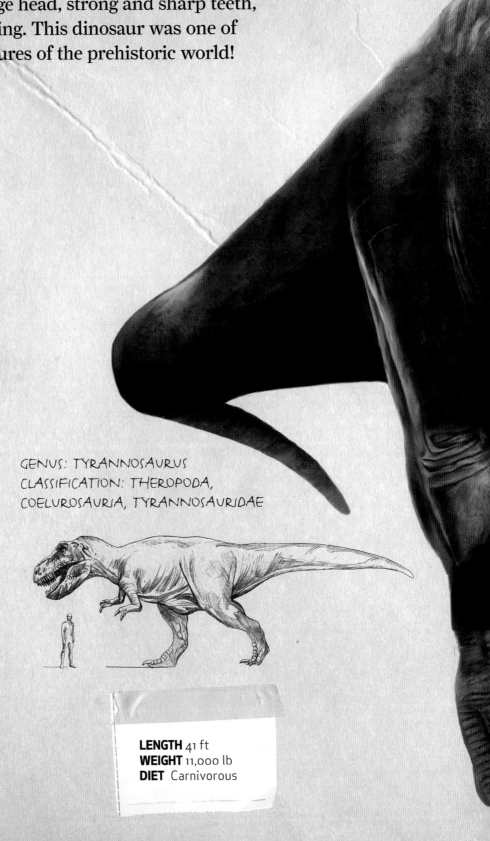

GENUS: TYRANNOSAURUS
CLASSIFICATION: THEROPODA, COELUROSAURIA, TYRANNOSAURIDAE

LENGTH 41 ft
WEIGHT 11,000 lb
DIET Carnivorous

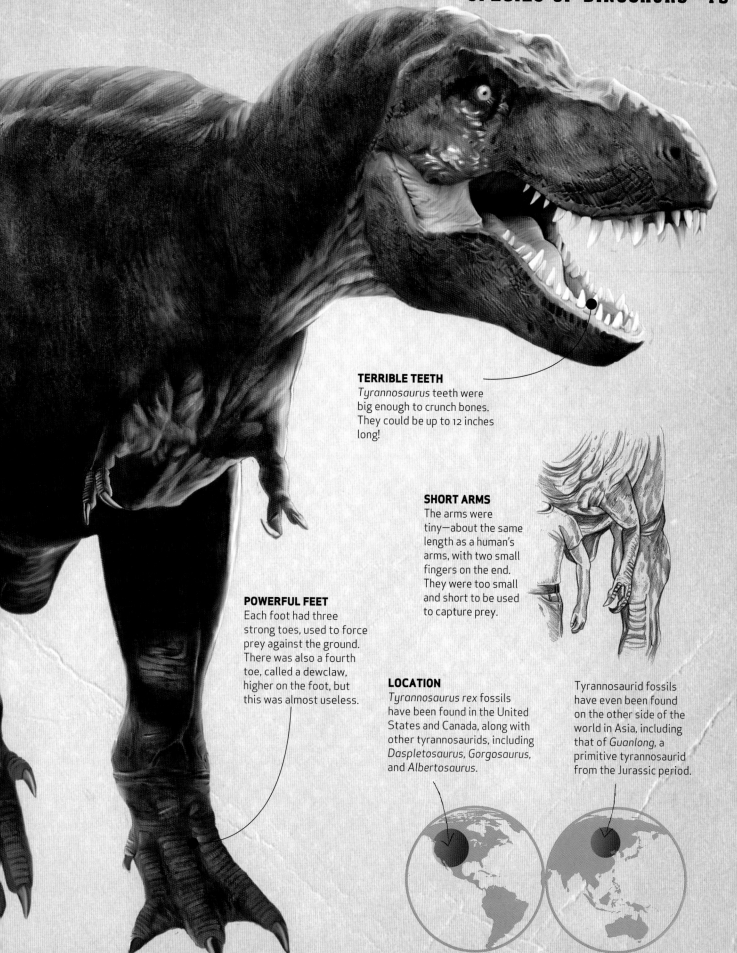

TERRIBLE TEETH
Tyrannosaurus teeth were big enough to crunch bones. They could be up to 12 inches long!

SHORT ARMS
The arms were tiny—about the same length as a human's arms, with two small fingers on the end. They were too small and short to be used to capture prey.

POWERFUL FEET
Each foot had three strong toes, used to force prey against the ground. There was also a fourth toe, called a dewclaw, higher on the foot, but this was almost useless.

LOCATION
Tyrannosaurus rex fossils have been found in the United States and Canada, along with other tyrannosaurids, including *Daspletosaurus*, *Gorgosaurus*, and *Albertosaurus*.

Tyrannosaurid fossils have even been found on the other side of the world in Asia, including that of *Guanlong*, a primitive tyrannosaurid from the Jurassic period.

Tyrannosaurus rex

FEROCIOUS TEETH
The teeth were rounded and
pointed, not blade-shaped as
in other theropods.

NAMING *TYRANNOSAURUS*
In 1905, Henry Fairfield
Osborn, a paleontologist at the
American Museum of Natural
History in New York, came up
with the name *Tyrannosaurus
rex.*

PHYLOGENETIC TREE

PERMIAN	252 mya	TRIASSIC	201 mya	JURASSIC	145 mya	CRETACEOUS	66 mya
				Coelosaurs		Tyrannosaurids	
				Tetanurans			
				Theropods			

SKELETON
The skeleton of *Tyrannosaurus rex* is believed to have around 200 bones.

PADDED FEET
Tyrannosaurus's three main toes had sharp claws. Underneath, they were padded to absorb impact against the ground.

Tyrannosaurus rex

FEATHERED BABY
A baby *Tyrannosaurus rex* probably had feathers, and many scientists think adults might have, too.

BIG HUNTER
It is thought that, due to its strength, *Tyrannosaurus* could bring down large herbivores.

LEGS
Tyrannosaurus's legs were long and muscular. Despite their weight, some scientists believe that these huge dinosaurs could still run to chase their prey.

HUGE HEAD
The head was 4.6 feet in length, and it had between 50 and 60 teeth in its mouth.

ARMS
They were so short that *Tyrannosaurus* couldn't even reach its own mouth!

Anatomy Characteristics

Fossils of dinosaur skeletons, teeth, footprints, eggs, and skin have given us huge amounts of information about the different kinds of dinosaurs. Paleontologists piece this information together with data about the dinosaurs' environment and about present-day species to build up a picture of the anatomy (body structure) of dinosaurs.

We know from the many fossilized dinosaur skeletons found that dinosaurs looked very similar to other reptiles. Bone structure, the scales that covered their bodies, and their birth from shelled eggs are key similarities.

Dinosaurs, however, had many features that were different from their reptile relatives, such as adaptations in their legs and hips, as they developed from crawling to an upright posture. During this process, a new arrangement of muscles evolved.

Most of the information we have about the body structure of dinosaurs comes from their bones, as these hard parts fossilized best. In a very few cases, impressions (marks on a surface) of dinosaur skin have been found. From these we know that some dinosaurs had hard coverings and small scales, while some recently discovered dinosaurs had feathery coverings. The study of present-day birds and reptiles also helps us to reconstruct the body posture of dinosaurs.

Ossified tendons (flexible cords that have changed into bone-like material)

Tibia (shinbone)

DEINONYCHUS SKELETON

The main features of the carnivorous dinosaur *Deinonychus* were similar to those of other theropods: a large skull, a short and curved neck, a strong backbone, and hind legs much longer than the front ones.

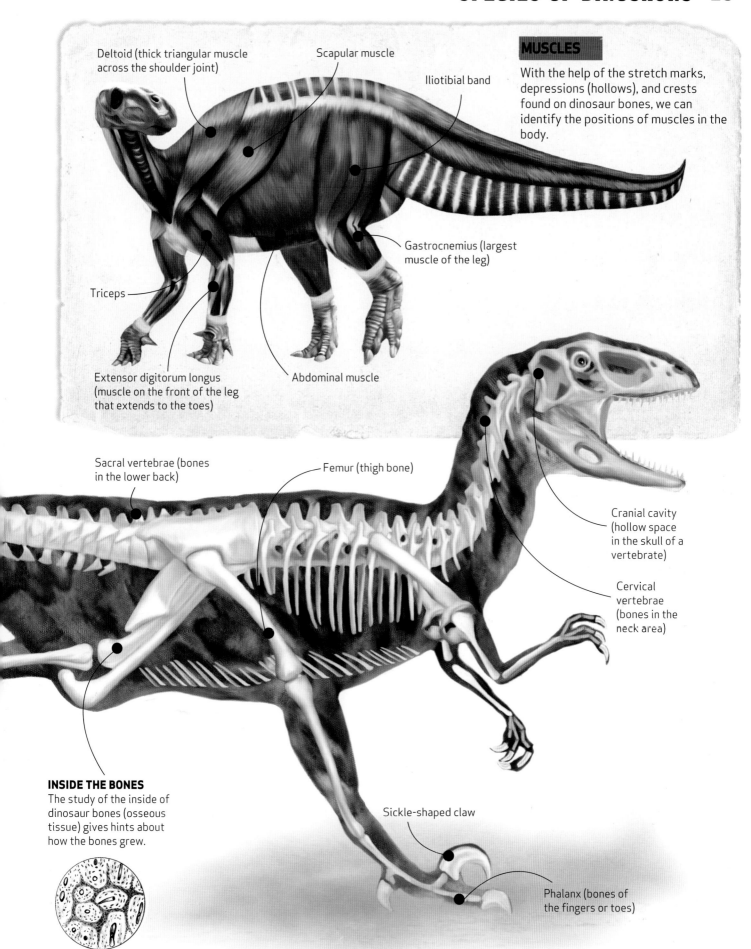

Deltoid (thick triangular muscle across the shoulder joint)

Scapular muscle

Iliotibial band

MUSCLES

With the help of the stretch marks, depressions (hollows), and crests found on dinosaur bones, we can identify the positions of muscles in the body.

Gastrocnemius (largest muscle of the leg)

Triceps

Extensor digitorum longus (muscle on the front of the leg that extends to the toes)

Abdominal muscle

Sacral vertebrae (bones in the lower back)

Femur (thigh bone)

Cranial cavity (hollow space in the skull of a vertebrate)

Cervical vertebrae (bones in the neck area)

INSIDE THE BONES
The study of the inside of dinosaur bones (osseous tissue) gives hints about how the bones grew.

Sickle-shaped claw

Phalanx (bones of the fingers or toes)

Inside a Dinosaur

CENTRAL CONTROL

The brains of herbivores were smaller than the brains of carnivores. A dinosaur's brain was located and protected inside the skull, just like ours, and different nerves pointed outward to collect information from the eyes, nose, mouth, and ear openings. The spinal cord started from the brain and extended through the backbone.

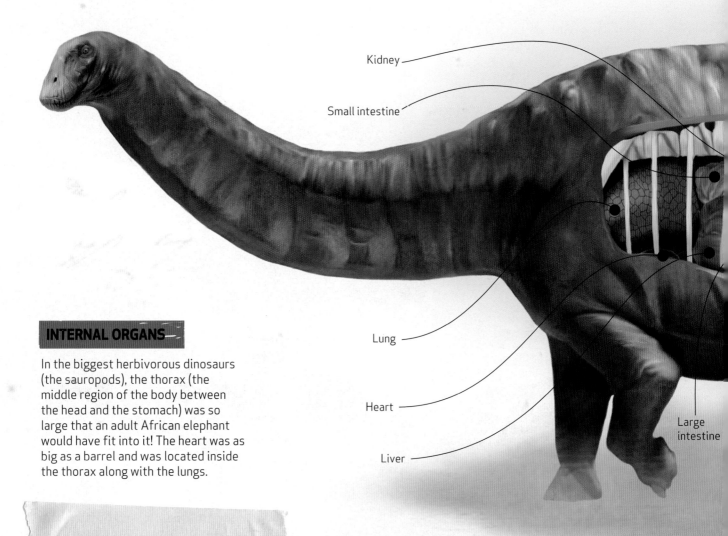

Kidney

Small intestine

Lung

Heart

Liver

Large intestine

INTERNAL ORGANS

In the biggest herbivorous dinosaurs (the sauropods), the thorax (the middle region of the body between the head and the stomach) was so large that an adult African elephant would have fit into it! The heart was as big as a barrel and was located inside the thorax along with the lungs.

SIZE AND WEIGHT

Dinosaurs were the group of reptiles with the widest range of sizes. Some dinosaurs, such as *Epidexipteryx*, were as tiny as sparrows. Others, including *Argentinosaurus*, were as big as blue whales!

SIZE COMPARISON
Many dinosaurs were small in size.

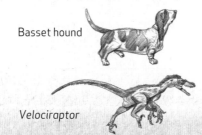

Basset hound

Velociraptor

WEIGHT COMPARISON
1 African elephant (11,905 lb) = 15 *Protoceratops*

SIZE COMPARISON

TYRANNOSAURUS
Tyrannosaurus had a brain smaller than that of humans.

STEGOSAURUS
Stegosaurus had a brain the size of a walnut.

TROODON
Troodon's brain was similar in size to that of *Tyrannosaurus rex*, but because it was large in relation to its head, it is thought to have been a more intelligent dinosaur.

Cloaca (reproductive and excretory opening)

Cecum (secondary digestion chamber to further break down food in order for the dinosaur to get essential nutrients from the plants it ate)

Muscular stomach

1 *Tyrannosaurus rex* (11,000 lb) = 1 African elephant

1 *Argentinosaurus* (160,000 lb) = 15 African elephants

Mesozoic Era

The 185-million-year span of the Mesozoic era is divided into three periods: Triassic, Jurassic, and Cretaceous. Dinosaurs were the most famous members of this era, which is often called "the era of the reptiles." But dinosaurs only began to appear at the end of the Triassic period, taking the place of the ancient reptiles.

The start of the Mesozoic era, around 250 million years ago, saw the extinction of huge numbers of the species that had inhabited Earth during the previous Paleozoic era. The creatures that did survive the extinction were sea dwellers. These included amniotes (four-legged, egg-laying creatures with backbones) and mollusks.

During the Mesozoic era itself, many organisms, including plants, invertebrates, and vertebrates, appeared and grew in number. In the oceans, gigantic reptiles, such as ichthyosaurs and plesiosaurs, fed on all types of fish. On the coasts and dry land, crocodiles, salamanders, and other reptiles grew in number and variety. In the middle of the Mesozoic era, dinosaurs began to make their appearance. Toward the end of the Triassic, as many other reptiles became extinct, the dinosaurs began to rule Earth.

VEGETATION
Gigantic conifers (cone-bearing trees) developed.

Pangaea

THE EARTH'S LANDMASSES

At the beginning of the Mesozoic era, the continental masses were gathered into a supercontinent, called Pangaea. During the Late Triassic, Pangaea began to separate into an upper part (Laurasia) and a lower part (Gondwana), divided by the Tethys Sea.

INVERTEBRATES
Grasshoppers appeared, and spiders and scorpions grew in number.

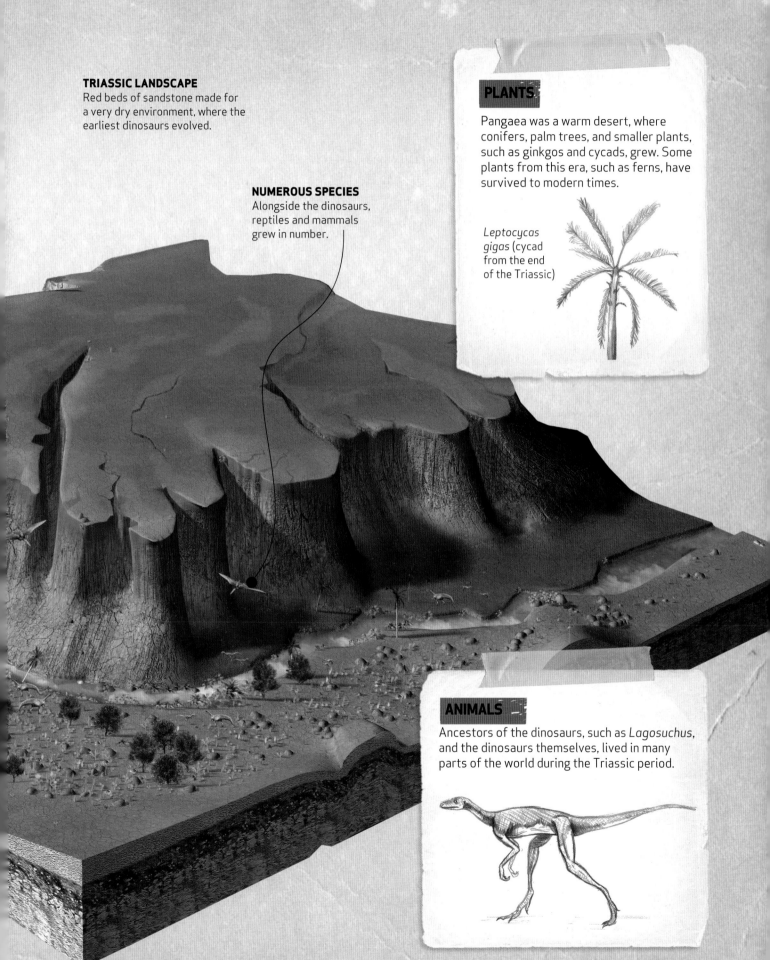

TRIASSIC LANDSCAPE
Red beds of sandstone made for a very dry environment, where the earliest dinosaurs evolved.

NUMEROUS SPECIES
Alongside the dinosaurs, reptiles and mammals grew in number.

PLANTS
Pangaea was a warm desert, where conifers, palm trees, and smaller plants, such as ginkgos and cycads, grew. Some plants from this era, such as ferns, have survived to modern times.

Leptocycas gigas (cycad from the end of the Triassic)

ANIMALS
Ancestors of the dinosaurs, such as *Lagosuchus*, and the dinosaurs themselves, lived in many parts of the world during the Triassic period.

The Ischigualasto Formation

Around 228 million years ago, in the south of Gondwana, the first dinosaurs lived alongside the last therapsids (mammal-like reptiles). The remains of these and other reptiles, together with amphibians, invertebrates, and plants, have been uncovered as fossils.

The Ischigualasto Provincial Park is one of the most important fossil sites of the Mesozoic era. Also known as the Valley of the Moon because of its desert landscape, it is located in San Juan, in the northwest of Argentina. It shows layers of rocky deposits from the entire 50 million years of the Triassic period that give us a unique fossil record of the period.

The first fossils found in Ischigualasto were collected in 1942. As well as dinosaur fossils, the formation includes reptile fossils. These support the theory that the dinosaurs and ancestors of mammals appeared gradually at the same time, and other reptiles then began to disappear.

Study of the rocks has revealed that the climate was extremely dry in the Early Triassic. However, during the middle of the Triassic the air was more humid, because many plants and animals have been preserved in the rock. Later, volcanic activity spread ashes that helped to preserve animal and plant life as fossils.

DICROIDIUM
Dicroidium was one of the most common plants in the Ischigualasto Formation. It grew among low-growing plants in forests and on flooded plains. It formed part of the green and bushy habitats of the Middle Triassic.

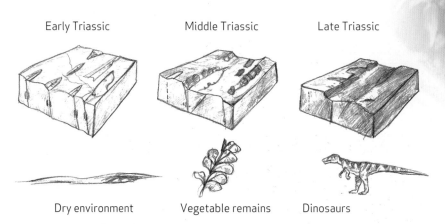

Early Triassic	Middle Triassic	Late Triassic
Dry environment	Vegetable remains	Dinosaurs

CARNIVORE OR OMNIVORE?
The small saurischian dinosaur *Eoraptor* might have been a carnivore (meat-eater) or an omnivore (plant- and meat-eater).

GIANT HERBIVORE
Ischigualastia was a massive, hippo-sized herbivorous therapsid.

TINY DINOSAUR
Pisanosaurus was a small ornithischian dinosaur, rare in the Triassic.

Dinosaur Ancestors

The Ischigualasto Formation has given us information about the oldest known species of dinosaurs. Fossils of *Herrerasaurus ischigualastensis* and *Eoraptor lunensis* that were found at Ischigualasto date back between 230 and 218 million years ago. From these and other fossils found in the formation, we have learned about the evolution of dinosaurs.

Ischigualasto has revealed fossils from the ancestors of birds, crocodiles, and lizards. Thousands of specimens have been collected, including the remains of the earliest dinosaur, *Eoraptor lunensis,* and its more advanced relative, the carnivorous *Herrerasaurus ischigualastensis.*

Most of the fossils have been found in the top levels of the formation and consist almost entirely of archosaurs. Archosaurs included the earliest ancestors of present-day crocodiles. *Saurosuchus galilei* was a type of archosaur known as a rauisuchian. It was a speedy carnivore that moved similarly to the crocodiles we know today.

Sillosuchus longicervix was also discovered in Ischigualasto. Its name comes from the Greek word *suchus,* meaning "crocodile."

SILLOSUCHUS LONGICERVIX

Related to present-day crocodiles, *Sillosuchus* had two long legs and lived on land. Its skeleton was light, which helped it to move fast.

ALL SIZES

The reptiles at Ischigualasto came in a wide variety of sizes. *Ischigualastia* was the size of a cow. There were also smaller forms, such as *Probainognathus*, which had a skull length of just 0.8 inch! Many of the fossils at Ischigualasto reveal supersized animals. *Saurosuchus*, an ancestor of the crocodiles, was almost 20 feet long. Among the dinosaurs, *Herrerasaurus* was the largest, with a body length of more than 10 feet.

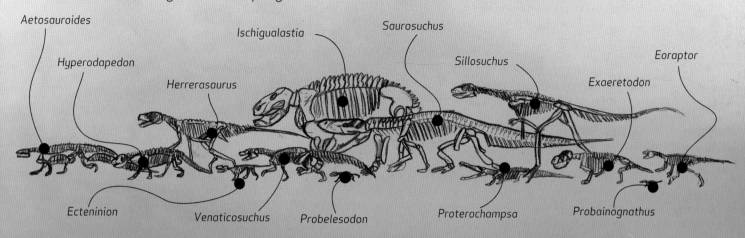

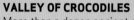

VALLEY OF CROCODILES
More than a dozen ancient crocodiles have been found at Ischigualasto, belonging to the Middle and Late Triassic.

MEAT-EATER
The largest carnivorous therapsid, *Chinicuodon theotonicus*, is known only from the remains of its skull.

Herrerasaurus

Herrerasaurus was a fast-moving carnivore that was well adapted for hunting herbivorous and omnivorous reptiles. Its remains have helped to provide important information about the origin and varied forms of dinosaurs.

H*errerasaurus* was one of the earliest known dinosaurs to be discovered, alongside others, such as *Eoraptor*, *Panphagia*, and *Staurikosaurus*. They were all found in rocks from the Triassic period, dating back approximately 228 million years.

Compared to reptiles at that time, *Herrerasaurus* was a rare species! It is classified as a saurischian theropod (a reptile-hipped dinosaur that was two-legged). It was one of the earliest meat-eating dinosaurs, with teeth of different sizes and shapes. The largest were very sharp and allowed *Herrerasaurus* to catch and kill prey. It also had big jaws, curved and pointed claws, and it could move at great speed. These features made it one of the most powerful hunters of the time.

GENUS: HERRERASAURUS
CLASSIFICATION: DINOSAURIA,
THEROPODA, HERRERASAURIDAE

LENGTH 10 ft
WEIGHT 463 lb
DIET Carnivorous

SKELETON
The skeleton of *Herrerasaurus* had a mixture of characteristics, some of which were similar to early reptiles, such as the two bones in its hip. Others were more advanced, dinosaur-like features, such as its ankle bones.

SHORT ARMS
The arms of *Herrerasaurus* were relatively short and are similar to those of later carnivorous dinosaurs. They had powerful claws to capture their prey.

LOCATION
Herrerasaurus was found in the Ischigualasto Provincial Park, in northwest Argentina. Remains of *Staurikosaurus* and *Sanjuansaurus*, also in the herrerasaurid family, have been found in the same place.

Herrerasaurus

In 1961, a team of explorers carried out a study in Ischigualasto. One of the team, Victorino Herrer, together with a local rancher and a collector, found a leg, a part of a hip, and most of the tailbones of a dinosaur. They also discovered many fragments of bones that belonged to the same species. From these remains, an Argentinian paleontologist, Osvaldo Reig, was able to describe *Herrerasaurus ischigualastensis*. He named it after its discoverer and the place it was found.

Herrerasaurus is now considered an "ancestral species" because it lived at a time when dinosaurs were still evolving. Its skeleton shows features midway between those of early reptiles and fully developed dinosaurs. It could run on two legs, unlike its ancestors, and so its arms and hands developed into efficient prey-grabbing tools, just like many later dinosaurs.

COMPARING ANCESTORS

In addition to *Herrerasaurus*, *Eoraptor* and *Pisanosaurus* were the other ancient animals of this time. They have all been the subject of much debate in attempting to place them on the evolutionary tree of the dinosaurs.

HIND LEGS

The structure of *Herrerasaurus*'s hind legs was very similar to its reptile ancestors.

PHYLOGENETIC TREE

PERMIAN		TRIASSIC		JURASSIC		CRETACEOUS	
	252 mya		201 mya		145 mya		66 mya

Archosaurs

Theropods

Saurischians

Hyperodapedon

Exaeretodon

POSSIBLE PREY
Herrerasaurus hunted therapsids such as *Hyperodapedon* and the slow-moving *Exaeretodon*. It might also have hunted smaller dinosaurs, such as *Eoraptor*, as well as amphibians and large insects of the Triassic.

JAW MOVEMENT
Herrerasaurus's jaws had a special joint that allowed them flexible movement to grasp their prey.

CLAWS
The claws on each finger were very sharp.

Herrerasaurus

MOVEMENT
Herrerasaurus had legs adapted for long strides. When running, its tail stuck out straight to balance the front of its body.

RECONSTRUCTION
The first complete jointed skeleton of *Herrerasaurus* was found in 1992. Before that date, it had been reconstructed from different pieces collected from different specimens.

MOUTH
Herrerasaurus had large jaws with many sawlike teeth that curved backward. These were specially adapted to its carnivorous diet.

FINGERS
The physical features of *Herrerasaurus*'s legs and hands, such as the outer fingers, were the same as those of ancient theropod dinosaurs.

Jurassic Period

The Jurassic period was the time when the biggest living creatures ever seen roamed the Earth. There were many different reptiles that lived on the land, in the sea, and in the sky. Large herbivorous and smaller carnivorous dinosaurs dominated the land.

D inosaurs grew to huge sizes in the Jurassic period. Sauropods (plant-eating dinosaurs), such as *Diplodocus* and *Brachiosaurus,* were among the largest. Other herbivorous species, such as the stegosaurs, developed fearsome body protection to fight large, powerful carnivores.

Alongside the larger dinosaurs were smaller, faster species that may have hunted in groups. *Archaeopteryx*, the first known bird, appeared toward the end of the Jurassic. It shared the skies with flying reptiles that had been on the planet since the Triassic.

In the oceans, ichthyosaurs and plesiosaurs lived with big sea crocodiles, sharks, rays, and various cephalopods (mollusks with tentacles, such as octopuses), which were similar to those alive today!

VEGETATION
Empty zones were soon covered up with trees.

PLANTS

There was plenty of rain during the Jurassic period, which resulted in rapid growth. Plants such as ferns and horsetails, as well as different species of conifer trees, formed thick forests.

Araucaria

Conifers

JURA
The name of this period comes from the Jura Mountains of France and Switzerland, where the first studies took place.

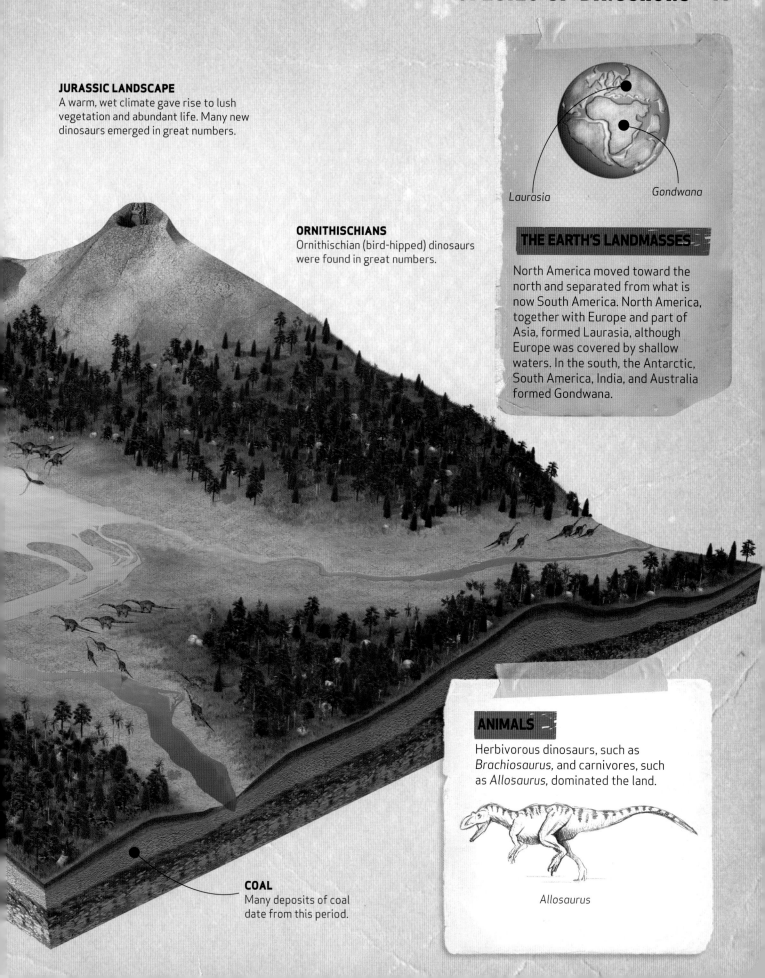

JURASSIC LANDSCAPE
A warm, wet climate gave rise to lush vegetation and abundant life. Many new dinosaurs emerged in great numbers.

ORNITHISCHIANS
Ornithischian (bird-hipped) dinosaurs were found in great numbers.

Laurasia   *Gondwana*

THE EARTH'S LANDMASSES

North America moved toward the north and separated from what is now South America. North America, together with Europe and part of Asia, formed Laurasia, although Europe was covered by shallow waters. In the south, the Antarctic, South America, India, and Australia formed Gondwana.

ANIMALS

Herbivorous dinosaurs, such as *Brachiosaurus*, and carnivores, such as *Allosaurus*, dominated the land.

Allosaurus

COAL
Many deposits of coal date from this period.

The Morrison Formation

Situated in the western United States, the Morrison Formation is one of the most amazing fossil sites in the world. Thousands of fossil remains of some of the best-known Jurassic dinosaurs have been found here.

The Morrison Formation is made up of rocks that were deposited over a span of eight million years in the Late Jurassic period. The first fossils were uncovered in 1877, and remarkable dinosaurs, such as *Stegosaurus*, *Diplodocus*, *Brachiosaurus*, and *Allosaurus,* were discovered.

We have also learned that, in the Late Jurassic, the climate in this region was warm and mostly dry. Rivers often dried up completely, but they could also flood suddenly after rainfall. Alongside the rivers grew low, soft plants, such as ferns, as well as trees. In the lakes and rivers, there were many varieties of fish and invertebrates, such as crabs, snails, and clams.

Frogs, lizards, tortoises, and crocodiles lived around the lakes. Pterosaurs (flying reptiles) searched for fish, and the first mammals also appeared here.

Among the many discoveries in the Morrison Formation was a fossil footprint trail. This has been the longest ever found, at about 2.5 miles in length!

ORIGINS
These rocks were formed by deposits on an enclosed area of water in the west of Pangaea. The constantly changing environment, with frequent river flooding and droughts, helped to fossilize bones.

HUGE DINOSAURS
From the fossils found in the Morrison Formation, we know that sauropods reached their maximum size in this region. This may have been due to seasonal rains and the resulting increased availability of sources of food, such as plants and trees.

FOSSIL WARS
At the end of the 19th century, the Morrison Formation had its own "bone wars," as paleontologists Othniel C. Marsh and Edward D. Cope competed for the discovery of the largest number of fossils!

NATURAL MONUMENT
One enormous block of rocks contains around 1500 fossilized bones, exactly as they were buried 150 million years ago during a river flood!

DROUGHT
The Jurassic environment could, at times, become extremely dry. In these extreme conditions, vegetation would have died out first, followed by the herbivorous dinosaurs, and then by the carnivores.

Efficient Hunters

Allosaurus was one of the largest hunters found in the Morrison Formation, reaching up to 40 feet in length.

Large carnivorous dinosaurs, such as *Allosaurus,* developed alongside the enormous herbivorous sauropods. These predators walked on two legs and had short arms with strong claws. It is possible that the carnivores evolved because they were able to take advantage of the large amount of available meat. Small, fast-moving carnivores, such as *Ornitholestes,* fed on animals smaller than themselves, or on leftovers.

TRACKING
The hunting scenes that took place here were recorded in footprints! There are many documented footprint trails that show carnivorous dinosaurs tracking sauropods.

ALLOSAURUS

Nearly 60 complete *Allosaurus* skeletons have been found in the Morrison Formation!

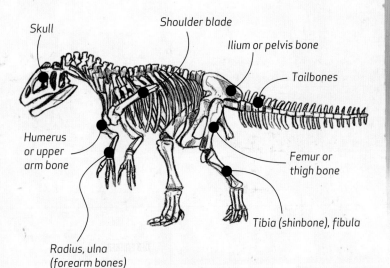

Skull

Shoulder blade

Ilium or pelvis bone

Tailbones

Humerus or upper arm bone

Femur or thigh bone

Radius, ulna (forearm bones)

Tibia (shinbone), fibula

STALKING THE PREY
The herbivore *Camptosaurus,* a close relative of the birdlike dinosaur *Iguanodon,* was prey for *Allosaurus.*

DIVERSITY OF CARNIVORES

A large number of different theropod dinosaurs have been found in the region—not only skeletons, but also fossilized footprints and droppings. More evidence comes from the teeth marks these predators imprinted in their victims' bones. *Allosaurus*, *Ceratosaurus*, and *Torvosaurus* are the best known of these carnivores.

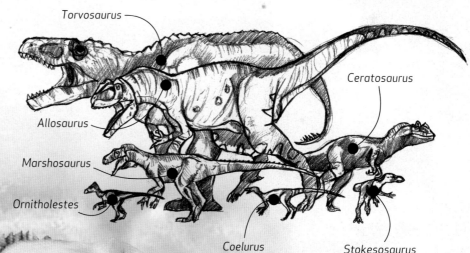

COMPARISON

The complete skeletons of many theropods have been found in the Morrison Formation. These discoveries have helped paleontologists to recreate the dinosaurs' body structures with great accuracy. *Torvosaurus* and *Allosaurus* were among the largest, while the smallest were *Stokesosaurus*, *Ornitholestes*, *Coelurus*, and *Tanycolagreus*.

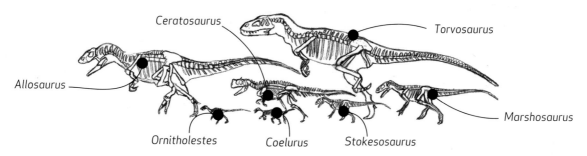

Stegosaurus

This armored dinosaur lived in North America 145 million years ago, but its relatives were found on many different continents. *Stegosaurus* ate low-lying plants that were digested in its massive stomach.

The beginning of the Jurassic period saw the appearance of animals that were two-legged and less than 3 feet in length. These were thyreophorans (meaning "shield bearers"). These birdlike dinosaurs had body coverings as protection or armor. The best known is *Scutellosaurus*, whose skin was protected by tiny shields of cone shapes. These small creatures were the forerunners of the stegosaurs and the ankylosaurs, which developed larger bodies and thicker, more complex armor.

The stegosaurs had armor along their necks, backs, and tails, in the form of large triangular plates and spikes. They were four-legged, with hooflike claws at the end of their toes. The most ancient stegosaur was *Huayangosaurus*, which was about 10 feet in length, but *Stegosaurus* reached up to 30 feet. At the beginning of the Cretaceous period, about 130 million years ago, these dinosaurs became extinct, possibly because of competition from new plant-eating species.

GENUS: STEGOSAURUS
CLASSIFICATION: ORNITHISCHIA, THYREOPHORA, STEGOSAURIDAE

LENGTH 30 ft
WEIGHT 11,000 lb
DIET Herbivorous

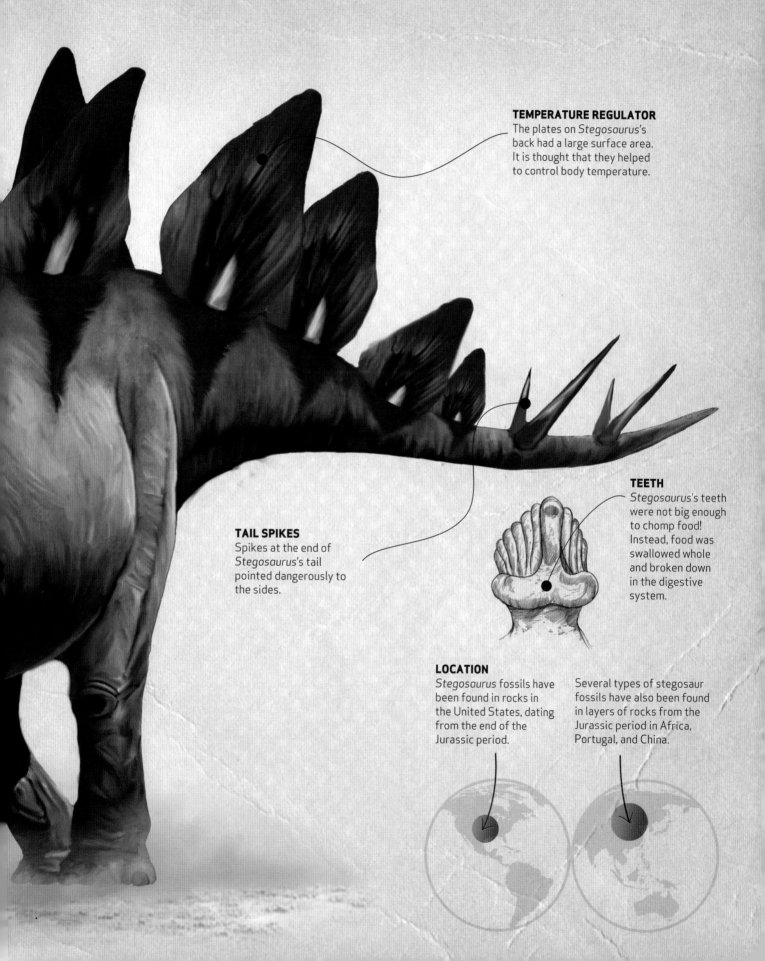

TEMPERATURE REGULATOR
The plates on *Stegosaurus*'s back had a large surface area. It is thought that they helped to control body temperature.

TEETH
Stegosaurus's teeth were not big enough to chomp food! Instead, food was swallowed whole and broken down in the digestive system.

TAIL SPIKES
Spikes at the end of *Stegosaurus*'s tail pointed dangerously to the sides.

LOCATION
Stegosaurus fossils have been found in rocks in the United States, dating from the end of the Jurassic period.

Several types of stegosaur fossils have also been found in layers of rocks from the Jurassic period in Africa, Portugal, and China.

Stegosaurus

Stegosaurs had five toes on their front feet and only three on their back feet. They carried their heads close to the ground, so that they could feed on low-lying plants.

The plates on a stegosaur's back were used in many ways. Firstly as armor for protection, but also for display and recognition, so members of the herd could communicate. The large plates had blood vessels near the surface, so they could have been used to control the temperature of the dinosaur's body.

At the end of *Stegosaurus*'s tail there were two pairs of long spikes used as a defensive weapon.

The brain cavity in the skull of *Stegosaurus* was very small, but there was a large area of the spinal cord at the hip area. This has led experts to suggest that this dinosaur might have had a "second brain."

LIFE AS A SAUROPOD

The stegosaurs roamed with great sauropods, such as *Diplodocus*, *Camarasaurus*, and *Apatosaurus*, at the end of the Jurassic period. They were always in danger of attack from carnivores, such as *Ceratosaurus* and *Allosaurus*.

PHYLOGENETIC TREE

PERMIAN	252 mya	TRIASSIC	201 mya	JURASSIC	145 mya	CRETACEOUS	66 mya
						Ankylosaurs	
		Ornithischians		Stegosaurs			
				Ornithopods			

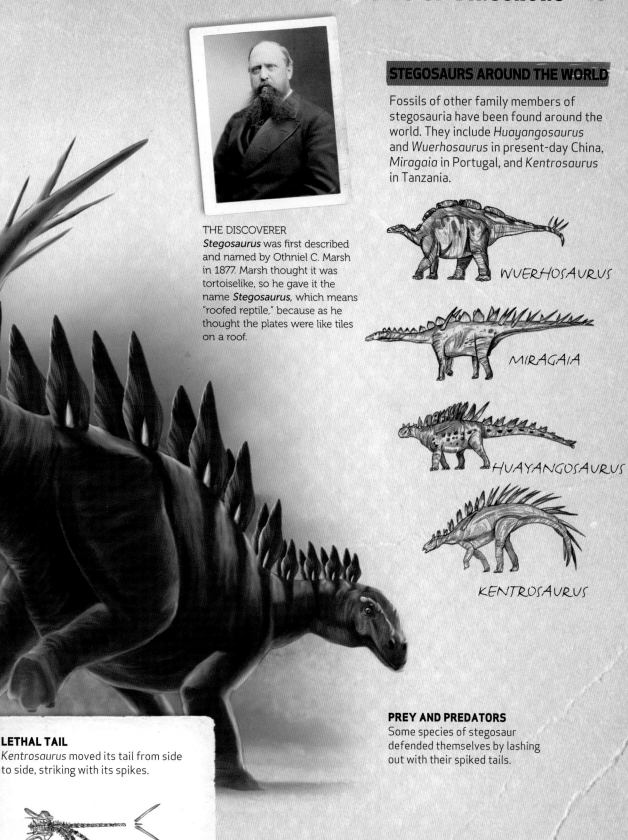

THE DISCOVERER
Stegosaurus was first described and named by Othniel C. Marsh in 1877. Marsh thought it was tortoiselike, so he gave it the name *Stegosaurus*, which means "roofed reptile," because as he thought the plates were like tiles on a roof.

STEGOSAURS AROUND THE WORLD

Fossils of other family members of stegosauria have been found around the world. They include *Huayangosaurus* and *Wuerhosaurus* in present-day China, *Miragaia* in Portugal, and *Kentrosaurus* in Tanzania.

WUERHOSAURUS

MIRAGAIA

HUAYANGOSAURUS

KENTROSAURUS

PREY AND PREDATORS
Some species of stegosaur defended themselves by lashing out with their spiked tails.

LETHAL TAIL
Kentrosaurus moved its tail from side to side, striking with its spikes.

Stegosaurus

BACK PLATES
The back plates were wide and thin, with an average height and width of approximately 25 inches.

HIPS
Stegosaurus had features similar to birdlike dinosaurs, with the forward portion of the hip bones pointing downward and backward.

SKELETON
The back was curved. The front legs were short, and the head was small and carried close to the ground. The tail was strong and held well above the ground.

SPIKES ON THE TAIL
Stegosaurus used this weapon well, pointing its tail directly toward its enemies.

Long-Necked Dinosaurs

Sauropod dinosaurs were the most gigantic animals ever to walk Earth. They spread throughout every corner of the world, and in Gondwana, they were the most common form of herbivores. Some of them reached a massive 115 feet in length!

Sauropods first appeared at the end of the Triassic period, around 200 million years ago. They became the dominant herbivores of the Mesozoic era and reached their peak during the Jurassic period.

The word *sauropod* means "footed lizard." The sauropods were given this name because of the five short toes on their back legs. These toes were very different from the slim feet of theropods and ornithopods, which were adapted for running. The sauropods were quadrupeds—they walked on four legs. Some could raise themselves up on their back legs to reach a treetop or to defend themselves.

Their heads were very small in relation to the rest of their bodies, and they had simple teeth of various types.

THE NECK
The sauropods had the longest necks of all dinosaurs and some species had up to 17 neck bones! Their long necks helped them see farther and be alert to danger. They also allowed them to reach into the treetops to find leaves and fruit. The bones (vertebrae) had air sacs to help support the long neck.

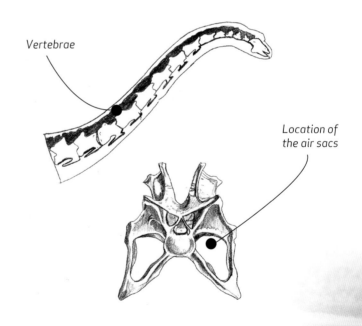

Vertebrae

Location of the air sacs

CHANGES IN POSTURE
Some sauropods may have been able to balance on their rear legs, supporting themselves with their tails, like a third leg!

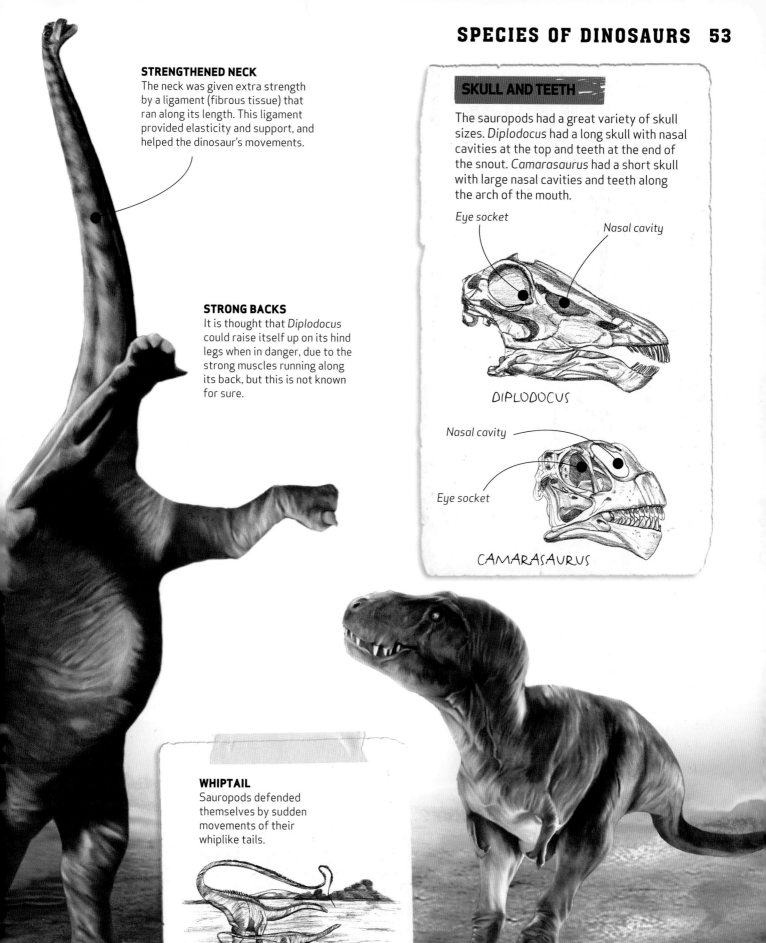

STRENGTHENED NECK
The neck was given extra strength by a ligament (fibrous tissue) that ran along its length. This ligament provided elasticity and support, and helped the dinosaur's movements.

STRONG BACKS
It is thought that *Diplodocus* could raise itself up on its hind legs when in danger, due to the strong muscles running along its back, but this is not known for sure.

WHIPTAIL
Sauropods defended themselves by sudden movements of their whiplike tails.

SKULL AND TEETH

The sauropods had a great variety of skull sizes. *Diplodocus* had a long skull with nasal cavities at the top and teeth at the end of the snout. *Camarasaurus* had a short skull with large nasal cavities and teeth along the arch of the mouth.

Eye socket

Nasal cavity

DIPLODOCUS

Nasal cavity

Eye socket

CAMARASAURUS

Diplodocids and Macronaria

The Late Jurassic period was the "golden age" of the sauropods. By that time, the two most important types in this group of herbivores were established: the diplodocids and macronaria.

The diplodocids had wide snouts with teeth at the end, somewhat like a rake! *Diplodocus* is the best known of all the diplodocids. Other species included *Brachytrachelopan*, which had a much shorter neck, and *Amargasaurus*, which had large spikes on its back.

The macronarian (large nose) sauropods included the biggest of them all—titanosaurs! These gigantic dinosaurs, including *Puertasaurus*, *Argentinosaurus*, and *Futalognkosaurus,* lived in South America during the Cretaceous period. They were the only sauropods to survive until the end of the Mesozoic era.

Titanosaurs measured between 100 and 115 feet in length. They all had a stronger skeleton structure than any other dinosaur group. Unlike diplodocids, they had shorter tails, which they used to support themselves on their hind legs.

Dreadnoughtus was a titanosaur first named in 2014. The fossils were of a young dinosaur, yet it was 85 feet long and weighed 72 tons.

EXCEPTIONAL

Brachytrachelopan was an exception among the sauropods because it was small in size and its neck was extremely short. It lived in Patagonia during the Jurassic period.

PROTECTION

Some titanosaurs, such as *Neuquensaurus*, had small plates on their backs. These plates formed a protective covering from predators like *Abelisaurus* and *Austroraptor*.

BIG AND SMALL

Brachytrachelopan was one of the smallest diplodocids, while *Diplodocus* was one of the largest.

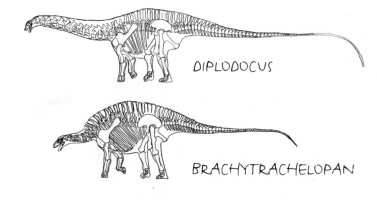

DIPLODOCUS

BRACHYTRACHELOPAN

BIGGEST GIANT

In the Cretaceous period, 90 million years ago, *Puertasaurus* lived in Patagonia. This massive dinosaur had a thick neck, which was able to move in every direction.

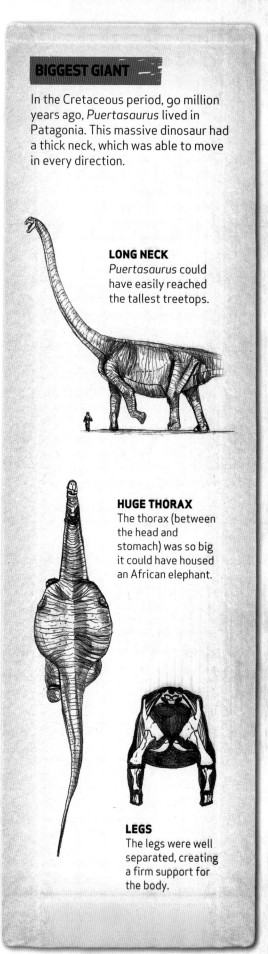

LONG NECK
Puertasaurus could have easily reached the tallest treetops.

HUGE THORAX
The thorax (between the head and stomach) was so big it could have housed an African elephant.

LEGS
The legs were well separated, creating a firm support for the body.

BODY STRUCTURE
Brachytrachelopan had a curved back and held its head close to the ground.

LIMITED DIET
Brachytrachelopan fed on low grasses because it could not reach up high.

Dilophosaurus

Dilophosaurus was made famous worldwide by the movie *Jurassic Park*. Its most notable feature was the double crest in the upper part of the skull.

Although *Jurassic Park* made *Dilophosaurus* famous, it also showed two features the dinosaur definitely did not have in real life—the ability to spit poison and the large fold of skin around the neck which opened like an umbrella!

Dilophosaurus was a member of a family of ancient two-legged dinosaurs that lived at the end of the Triassic period and beginning of the Jurassic. Its remains have been found in both North America and Asia. This shows that *Dilophosaurus* was present in large numbers in various places as the Pangaea supercontinent was being formed.

Among the ancient relatives of *Dilophosaurus* were *Coelophysis*, *Megapnosaurus*, *Liliensternus*, and *Zupaysaurus*. All of them had a long skull, with many teeth. The snout was partly separated from the rest of the head. The neck was thin and very flexible, which meant it could be stretched quickly to allow the dinosaur to catch prey in its mouth.

GENUS: DILOPHOSAURUS
CLASSIFICATION: THEROPODA, COELOPHYSOIDEA

LENGTH 20 ft
WEIGHT 1,100 lb
DIET Carnivorous

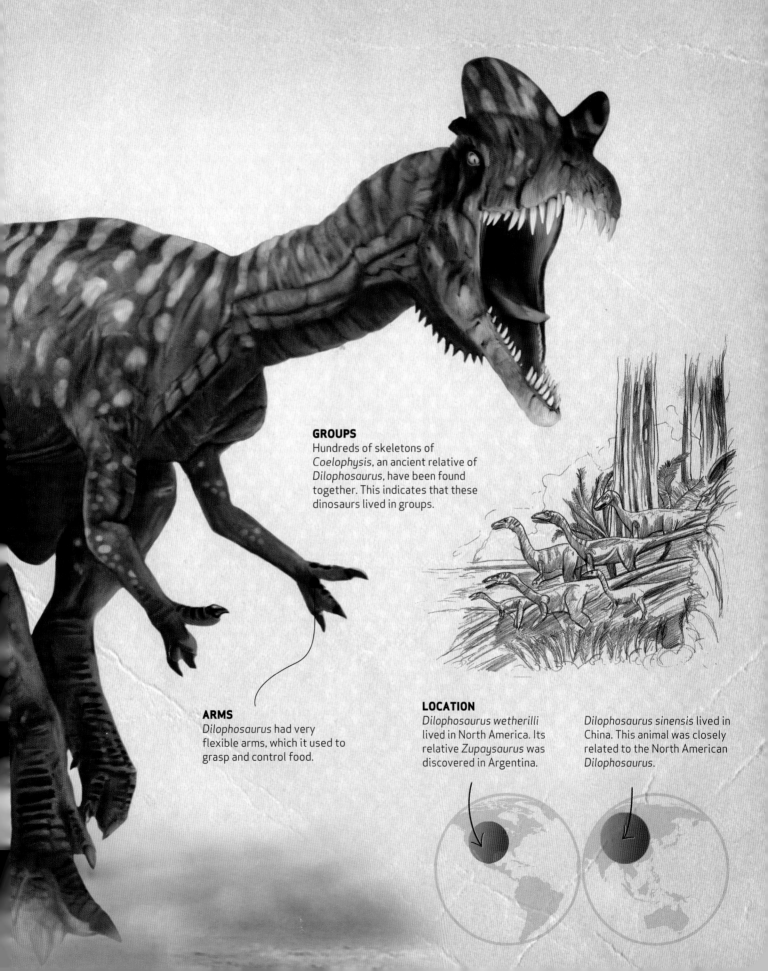

GROUPS
Hundreds of skeletons of *Coelophysis*, an ancient relative of *Dilophosaurus*, have been found together. This indicates that these dinosaurs lived in groups.

ARMS
Dilophosaurus had very flexible arms, which it used to grasp and control food.

LOCATION
Dilophosaurus wetherilli lived in North America. Its relative *Zupaysaurus* was discovered in Argentina.

Dilophosaurus sinensis lived in China. This animal was closely related to the North American *Dilophosaurus*.

Dilophosaurus

Dilophosaurus was one of the largest theropods of the early Jurassic period, reaching up to 20 feet in length. Its name means "two lophos (crests) reptile," since its most obvious characteristic was the complex structure of crests on its head. They were only a few millimeters thick, and it is thought that they may have been used for communication and recognition, similar to how roosters use their fleshy "combs" today.

At the beginning of the Jurassic period, *Dilophosaurus* was the most dangerous predator, because there were no other large-sized carnivores around at that time.

OTHER PRIMITIVE DINOSAURS

The theropod *Coelophysis* and the ornithischian *Scutellosaurus* lived together in North America, 190 million years ago. *Scutellosaurus* was a small dinosaur and a distant relative of ankylosaurs and stegosaurs.

SCUTELLOSAURUS

COELOPHYSIS

PHYLOGENETIC TREE

PERMIAN	252 mya	TRIASSIC	201 mya	JURASSIC	145 mya	CRETACEOUS	66 mya

Dilophosaurus

Theropods

Tetanurans

SKELETON
Skeletons of *Dilophosaurus* have been preserved in excellent condition! They provide us with important data about the body structure of the ancient theropods.

THE DISCOVERER
In 1942, U.S. paleontologist Samuel P. Welles found an almost complete skeleton of *Dilophosaurus*. Some years later, another one was found with an almost intact skull.

Dilophosaurus

LONG TAIL
Dilophosaurus had a large number of bones in its tail. The main function of the tail was to balance the body.

HANDS
Dilophosaurus had three fingers with claws and a fourth one that was smaller in size. This set the pattern for the structure of the hands of future theropods.

LEGS
The legs of *Dilophosaurus* were long and muscular. They had three toes facing forward and another smaller one pointing to the side. *Dilophosaurus* ran very fast on its hind legs.

SKULL
The skull was long, with two crests down the center of the top. It had wide openings for the nasal cavities and eye sockets.

CREST
The head was topped with two delicate crests. They may have been colorful and were probably used to help animals recognize each other.

NECK
Dilophosaurus had a long, S-shaped neck, similar to birds today. When the animal was alert or sensed danger, it held its head high to look out over its territory.

Cretaceous Period

The Cretaceous period was the longest period in the Mesozoic era, lasting around 80 million years (145 to 66 million years ago). Large numbers of dinosaurs of many different sizes and shapes roamed Earth. Enormous pterosaurs flew in the skies alongside the birds, and there were many small insects such as bees and moths.

The Cretaceous period was a time of warm, humid climates with no ice caps covering the poles. This meant that sea levels were high, with many of the continents covered in warm, shallow waters. There was an explosion of different life forms in this period. Flowering plants appeared, and the dinosaurs continued to develop in many varied forms. These included horned dinosaurs, such as *Triceratops*, small dinosaurs, such as *Velociraptor*, and giant carnivores, such as *Tyrannosaurus rex*.

The Cretaceous period—and the Mesozoic era—ended with a massive extinction that saw all the big animals, including the dinosaurs, perish. Scientists believe that this extinction was caused by increased volcanic activity (eruptions), together with one or more meteorites colliding with Earth. They think that the dust and ash from these events reduced the amount of sunlight reaching Earth, with catastrophic results for plants and animals.

PLANTS

Flowering plants appeared around 100 million years ago. They grew alongside the seed-bearing trees (such as conifers), which had dominated the Mesozoic era up to that time.

FORESTS
Forests flourished in areas with humid climates and then spread to other parts.

CRETACEOUS LANDSCAPE
This period had a relatively warm climate, resulting in high sea levels and shallow inland seas.

MOUNTAINS
Mountain ranges such as the Alps in Europe began to form during the Cretaceous period.

EARTH'S LANDMASSES
The positions of the landmasses on planet Earth were similar to their positions today. North America and Europe, Africa, and South America separated. As the two American plates moved to the west, they collided with the Pacific Ocean plate, pushing land up at the plate edges to create huge mountain ranges.

ANIMALS
Although dinosaurs ruled the world during the Cretaceous period, many mammals also evolved during this time. *Repenomamus*, found in the north of China, was one of the largest mammals of the Mesozoic era.

SUCCESSFUL DINOSAURS
Dinosaurs existed in huge numbers and varieties during this period, and they spread around the world.

The Gobi Desert

The Gobi Desert, in the heart of Asia, is famous all over the world for the large quantity of well-preserved dinosaur remains that have been found there. Exploration of this region began early in the 20th century.

An enormous number of vertebrate fossils have been found in the Gobi Desert. The fossils are well preserved, which has led paleontologists to wonder if a natural disaster may have buried the animals very suddenly.

The first expedition to the Gobi Desert was led by an American explorer, Roy Chapman Andrews, in the 1920s. The first fossilized dinosaur eggs were discovered in Flaming Cliffs, one of the most celebrated sites in the Gobi Desert. The rocks of Flaming Cliffs were formed in an extremely dry climate. Dozens of well-preserved eggs were found here, some with parts of the shell intact!

Because the most common species at this site was *Protoceratops*, it was thought that these were *Protoceratops* eggs. A different dinosaur found buried on top of a clutch of eggs was assumed to be a predator. This animal was named *Oviraptor*, which means "egg thief."

However, new research in the 1980s proved that the eggs belonged to *Oviraptor* and not *Protoceratops*!

MARKS FROM THE PAST
Many dinosaur footprints have been found in Gobi Desert rocks. One of them is thought to be a footprint of *Protoceratops*.

A GOBI EXPLORER
Roy Chapman Andrews led several expeditions to the Gobi Desert, organized and funded by the American Museum of Natural History in New York.

FLAMING CLIFFS
Dozens of fossilized egg remains were found in this location. Although *Protoceratops* may have built raised nests here, it is now thought that most of the eggs found at Flaming Cliffs belonged to *Oviraptor*.

Origin of Birds

The origin of birds has been much debated. Many paleontologists today believe that birds are related to flesh-eating, two-legged dinosaurs. The two groups have similarities in bones, eggs, and behavior. The discovery of spectacular fossils in China prove that many dinosaurs had feathers. The most detailed studies point to maniraptorans (a group that includes oviraptors) being the direct ancestors of birds.

REPTILIAN INHERITANCE

Maniraptors and theropods have a lot of physical similarities to birds, as seen on the skeleton.

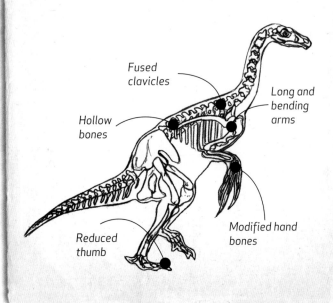

Fused clavicles

Long and bending arms

Hollow bones

Reduced thumb

Modified hand bones

INCUBATING

Some oviraptorid skeletons have been found on top of nests. This proved that dinosaurs sat on their eggs to provide warmth and to help them hatch.

ROOSTER MIMIC
The theropod *Gallimimus* looked like an ostrich. Its name means "rooster mimic."

FEATHER COVERAGE
Bones with tiny swellings, found in 2007, show that *Velociraptor* definitely had feathers!

FEATHER EVOLUTION

In the beginning, the purpose of feathers was to maintain body heat. Later on, they became useful for flying.

Growing bud from inside a pod	Strands appear in the bud	Branched outgrowths develop	Hooks appear in the outgrowths	Feathers are similar to those of today

Beipiaosaurus	*Sinosauropteryx*	*Sinornithosaurus*	*Caudipteryx*	*Archaeopteryx*

Spinosaurus

An extraordinary predator that hunted on land and in water, *Spinosaurus* was one of the most gigantic theropods ever to walk on Earth.

Some paleontologists believe that *Spinosaurus* reached up to 60 feet in length and around 9 tons in weight, leaving both *Tyrannosaurus rex* and *Giganotosaurus* behind! Discoveries made in countries such as Niger, Morocco, Britain, and Brazil have provided us with information about the structure and lifestyle of these amazing dinosaurs. Other notable features include a massive skull, nearly 6 feet long, and rows of spines on the back, which measured up to 5.5 feet!

The spinosaurids were a special type of theropod, with long snouts and cone-shaped teeth like those of crocodiles. The digested remains of fish scales and bones, as well as the remains of a young *Iguanodon*, have been found inside the ribs of fossils of the spinosaurid *Baryonyx*. In Brazil, the mark of a *Spinosaurus* tooth was discovered on a neck bone of a pterosaur, a flying reptile. From this and other evidence, it's clear that the spinosaurid's diet included fish, young herbivorous dinosaurs, and flying reptiles.

Recent studies reveal that *Spinosaurus aegypticus* was a semiaquatic dinosaur, with short, powerful hind legs adapted for paddling in water.

GENUS: SPINOSAURUS
CLASSIFICATION: THEROPODA, TETANURAE, SPINOSAURIDAE

LENGTH 41—60 ft
WEIGHT 11,000—20,000 lb
DIET Carnivorous

LEGS
They were strong enough to support the body weight, which was increased by the extra weight of the spiny back.

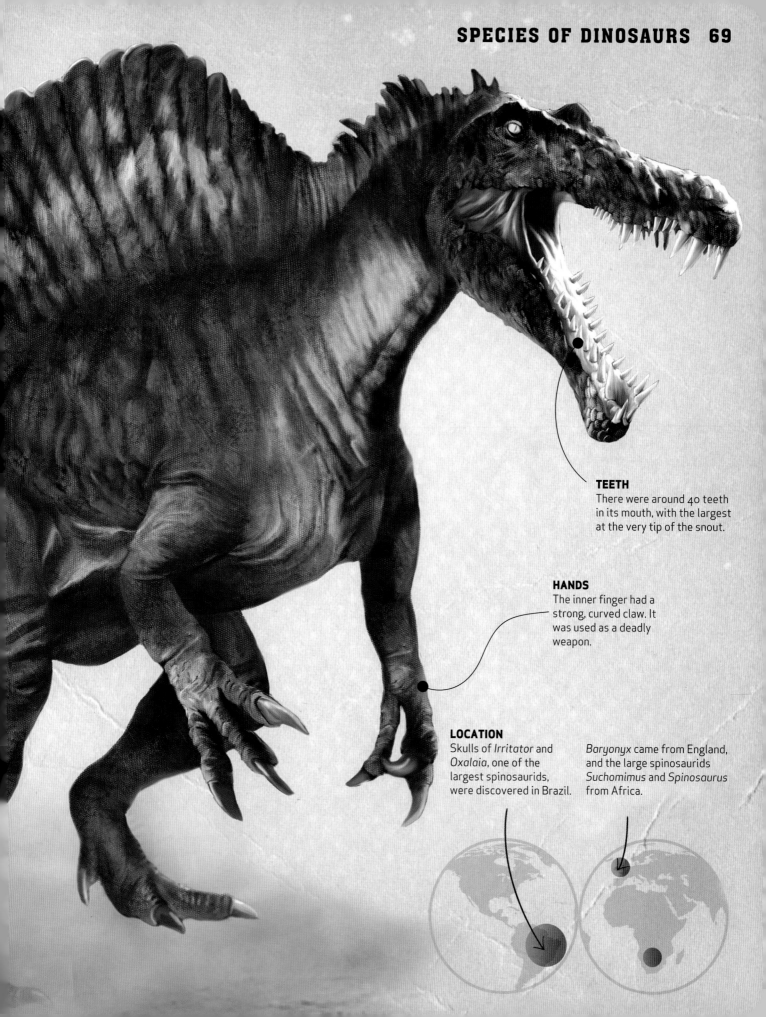

TEETH
There were around 40 teeth in its mouth, with the largest at the very tip of the snout.

HANDS
The inner finger had a strong, curved claw. It was used as a deadly weapon.

LOCATION
Skulls of *Irritator* and *Oxalaia*, one of the largest spinosaurids, were discovered in Brazil.

Baryonyx came from England, and the large spinosaurids *Suchomimus* and *Spinosaurus* from Africa.

Spinosaurus

Spinosaurus was well suited to catching fish. Its skull has similarities to that of crocodiles, at the edges of the mouth and in the shape of the teeth. Like crocodiles, *Spinosaurus* may have had pressure sensors at the tip of the snout that helped it to detect prey moving in water. This meant that it could strike at fish without being able to see them!

The huge spines running along its back have confused paleontologists. Could they have formed a kind of "sail"? A sail would have helped to control body temperature by taking in heat when the animal was facing the sun. However, recent studies suggest that the spines on the back supported a large hump of fat, similar to those on camels or bison. This hump would have stored energy to allow the dinosaur to survive during times when there was little food or water.

Spinosaurus shared the environment with other carnivores, such as *Carcharodontosaurus*. But it seems that they did not compete for food resources. *Spinosaurus* fed mainly on fish, while *Carcharodontosaurus* fed on land-based, herbivorous dinosaurs.

THE DISCOVERER
In 1912, the German paleontologist Ernst Stromer found the first remains of *Spinosaurus* in Egypt. Unfortunately, this skeleton was destroyed in a bombing raid during World War II.

PHYLOGENETIC TREE

PERMIAN	252 mya	TRIASSIC	201 mya	JURASSIC	145 mya	CRETACEOUS	66 mya
						Spinosaurids	
				Tetanurans			
		Theropods					
						Coelurosaurs	

GOOD SWIMMER?

To be able to find and catch its prey effectively, *Spinosaurus* was probably a good swimmer.

Flapping tail

SKELETON

The skeleton shows that *Spinosaurus* was a biped, but it may have crouched or rested on all four limbs.

Spinosaurus

LONG HEAD
Spinosaurus's head had a narrow snout with a hooklike tip and many sharp, pointed teeth.

TEETH
The teeth of *Spinosaurus* were cone-shaped and less curved than those in other theropods. They are similar to the teeth of modern-day crocodiles.

ARMS
Spinosaurus had long, strong arms, very different from those of the tyrannosaurids. The fingers on the hands had highly developed claws.

SAIL
The spines that supported the sail were massive—over 10 times longer than the diameter of the vertebrae that they grew from.

Suchomimus

Suchomimus was a fish-eating dinosaur that spent most of its time in or near water. It also captured other dinosaurs and pterosaurs. This behavior and some of its physical features make it similar to present-day crocodiles.

This dinosaur's fossils were found in rocks of the Late Cretaceous in Niger, Africa. The specimen was between 36 and 40 feet in length, which makes it one of the largest known theropods.

The structure of *Suchomimus* is similar to other dinosaurs of that period, including *Irritator* and *Oxalaia*, both of which were found in Brazil in South America. This is not surprising as, 120 million years ago, Africa was closer to South America than it is today. This meant that dinosaurs, crocodiles, and freshwater fish could have moved from one continent to another.

Suchomimus had around 100 cone-shaped teeth, which had crests that locked firmly and allowed the dinosaur to grip slippery fish. The head was long and carried low, with nasal cavities higher than the tip of the snout to keep them above water when the snout was beneath the surface.

GENUS: SUCHOMIMUS
CLASSIFICATION: THEROPODA, TETANURAE, SPINOSAURIDAE

LENGTH 40 ft
WEIGHT 11,000 lb
DIET Carnivorous

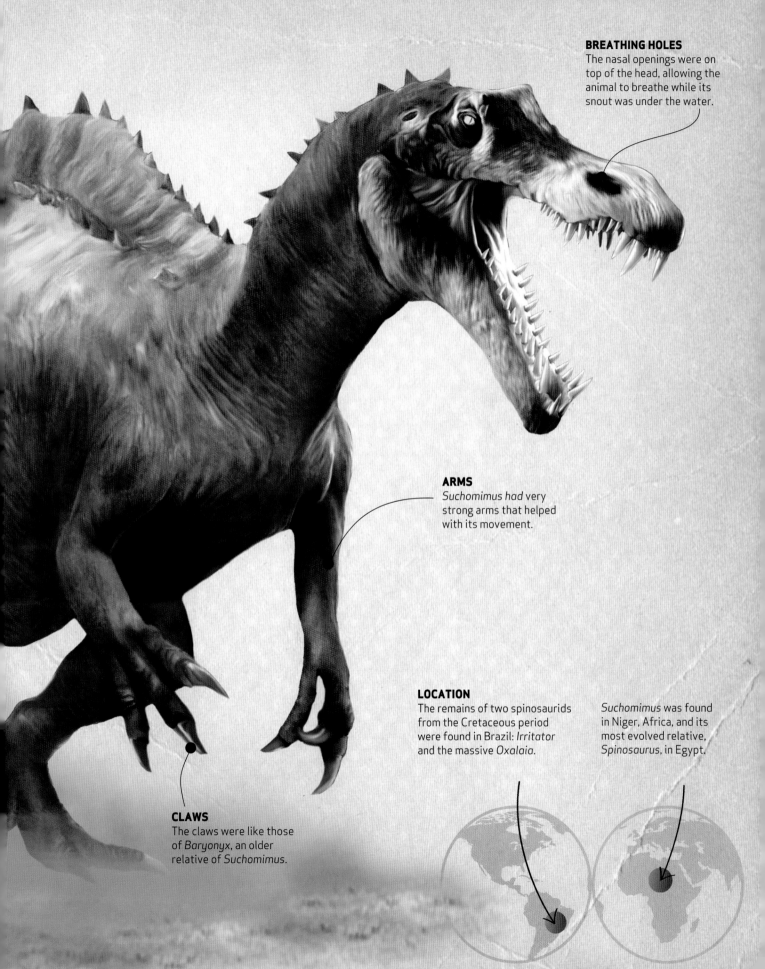

BREATHING HOLES
The nasal openings were on top of the head, allowing the animal to breathe while its snout was under the water.

ARMS
Suchomimus had very strong arms that helped with its movement.

LOCATION
The remains of two spinosaurids from the Cretaceous period were found in Brazil: *Irritator* and the massive *Oxalaia*.

Suchomimus was found in Niger, Africa, and its most evolved relative, *Spinosaurus*, in Egypt.

CLAWS
The claws were like those of *Baryonyx*, an older relative of *Suchomimus*.

Suchomimus

Suchomimus had neural spines along its back, but they were lower than in *Spinosaurus*. It is thought that these carnivorous dinosaurs carried a hump of energy-storing fat on their backs. Evidence indicates that their main source of food was fish but, like *Spinosaurus*, *Suchomimus* would catch and eat other animals if necessary.

An interesting adaptation of *Suchomimus* was the huge sickle-shaped claw on its thumb. All the arm bones were very strong, indicating that the limbs were useful for movement and hunting.

THE DISCOVERER
Suchomimus was found by Paul Sereno of the University of Chicago in Illinois, during a scientific expedition to the Sahara in 1997.

PHYLOGENETIC TREE

PERMIAN	252 mya	TRIASSIC	201 mya	JURASSIC	145 mya	CRETACEOUS	66 mya
						Spinosaurids	
				Tetanurans		Carnosaurs	
		Theropods				Coelurosaurs	

DIET
The structure of *Suchomimus*'s jaws, together with the shape of its teeth and the fossilized contents of its stomach, suggests that its main prey was fish. It may have eaten fish like this *Lepidotes*.

CROCODILE MIMIC
Suchomimus got its name from its skull, which is like that of a crocodile, with a long, low snout.

ARMS
Suchomimus had long arms, with large, curved claws on the hands.

Suchomimus

HUMP
The spinal bones on the back supported a hump similar to a camel's. They were shorter than those of *Spinosaurus*, the gigantic descendant of *Suchomimus*.

STRONG LEGS
Suchomimus used its strong legs for plunging into rivers to catch fish, and probably for swimming also.

SKULL
The skull of *Suchomimus* was over 3 feet in length.

SNOUT
Suchomimus had a long, narrow snout. Its teeth were arranged in a similar way to those of modern-day gharials (a type of crocodile).

SKELETON
The first discovery of a complete skeleton of *Suchomimus* was of a young animal that was not fully developed. When fully grown, it would have been similar in size to a *Tyrannosaurus*.

Herbivores

Herbivorous species appeared early in the history of dinosaurs. The sauropodomorphs and ornithischians were the most common herbivores of the Mesozoic era.

At the end of the Triassic period, the two main groups of herbivorous dinosaurs appeared: the sauropodomorphs and the ornithischians. The early members of each group were small, and they shredded plants with their leaf-shaped teeth. Gradually some sauropodomorphs grew in size. Their sauropod descendants included the long-necked *Diplodocus* and *Nigersaurus*.

Ornithischians were smaller than the sauropods, and fed on different plant matter. Iguanodonts became important members of this dinosaur family, and in the Cretaceous period, they were the most common and widespread of the herbivores. The ornithischians also included the hadrosaurs, larger dinosaurs, such as *Ankylosaurus* and *Stegosaurus*, and those with complex skulls, such as the ceratopsians.

Therizinosaurs were theropods that fed on plants instead of meat.

HEAD OF *NIGERSAURUS*

The skull of *Nigersaurus* was adapted for very efficient grazing. It held its head low, and its light skull made this easier. It chopped and swallowed vegetation quickly with its 500 to 600 teeth. Because the vegetation was tough, the teeth frequently regrew as they wore out.

Spade-shaped jaws

Light skull

HERBIVOROUS TOOTH
Many herbivorous dinosaurs had small teeth with sawlike edges. They used these teeth to chop their leafy food into smaller and smaller pieces before swallowing, so that they could then digest more quickly.

NANSHIUNGOSAURUS
This weird therizinosaur from China had a long neck that ended in a small head.

GRAZING AT DIFFERENT HEIGHTS

Sauropods could reach the young leaves of taller trees, while the smaller ornithischians fed from lower branches and bushes.

ANCIENT ORNITHISCHIAN
Pisanosaurus is the oldest known ornithischian. It lived in Argentina at the end of the Triassic period.

DEFENSE
Like present-day sloths, therizinosaurs defended themselves with their long, sharp claws.

One of the main sources of food for herbivorous dinosaurs were seed-producing plants, such as ginkgos, pines, and araucarias, and cycads. These plants flourished in the Mesozoic era, and both sauropods and ornithischians fed on them. They also ate plants such as ferns, because they grew at ground level and were easy to reach, even for baby dinosaurs.

Flowering plants also flourished in the Cretaceous period and soon became dominant in many environments. Because these plants were seasonal, the leaves were less tough compared to most conifers whose leaves lasted many years. Dinosaurs soon started feeding on this new vegetation and helped the plants to reproduce quickly by spreading the seeds around via their droppings. However, herbivorous dinosaurs did have to adapt to this new food, so there were changes to their teeth and digestive systems.

FOSSIL PLANT
Bennettitales was a group of plants that were common in the Jurassic period and at the beginning of the Cretaceous period, before becoming extinct toward the end of the Cretaceous period. Some of them looked like ferns today. This photograph shows a fossilized leaf from the Jurassic period.

Giant Stomachs

Ankylosaurus had perhaps the largest stomach of all the herbivorous dinosaurs. This is indicated by the low, wide shape of the body. It is believed that the animal developed this structure to help it get the maximum amount of nourishment from the leaves and fruits it consumed. These animals did not grind the food; instead, it was softened and broken up by their well-developed digestive system.

CHEEKS
Ankylosaurus had fleshy cheeks similar to those of mammals, which helped it to keep the food inside its mouth.

MOUTH
Ankylosaurus's teeth were tiny, heart-shaped, and formed rows at the edges of the mouth.

DIGESTIVE ADAPTATIONS

Ankylosaurus, the iguanodonts, and ceratopsians fully digested the food they ate, which helped their growth.

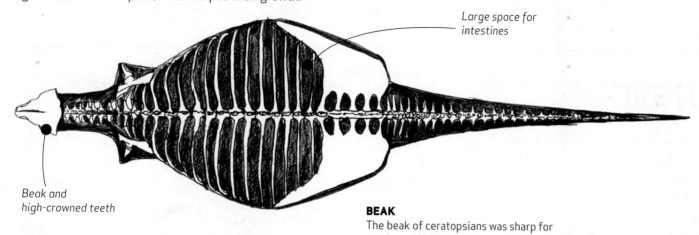

Large space for intestines

Beak and high-crowned teeth

BEAK

The beak of ceratopsians was sharp for cutting and biting tough vegetation.

Iguanodon

Large numbers of *Iguanodon* fossils have been found in many different parts of the world. From this evidence, we know that they formed groups, roaming together in search of food.

Iguanodon, meaning "iguana tooth," was a dinosaur that lived in Europe in the Middle Cretaceous period, some 125 million years ago. It was a large, strong herbivore that moved on either two or four legs, resting its hooflike fingers on the ground.

Adult animals measured around 33 feet in length, although some could reach up to 43 feet. The skull was tall, with a narrow snout ending in a toothless beak.

Although first found in England in 1822, the most extraordinary discovery of *Iguanodon* remains came from a coal mine at Bernissart in Belgium, in 1878. Bones from 38 animals were gathered from this mine, allowing the Belgian paleontologist Louis Dollo to assemble several skeletons and learn more about these spectacular dinosaurs.

GENUS: IGUANODON
CLASSIFICATION: ORNITHISCHIA, ORNITHOPODA, IGUANODONTIA

LENGTH 33 ft
WEIGHT 11,000 lb
DIET Herbivorous

CHEWING
The structure of the beak, together with the movement of its jaw, helped *Iguanodon* to grind up its food.

LOCATION
Remains of *Iguanodon* have been found in Europe, and the unusual iguanodont *Ouranosaurus* was discovered in Africa.

Iguanodon

The iguanodonts are grouped together within the Ornithopoda category. The name *Ornithopoda*, meaning "bird foot," comes from the fact that many dinosaurs in this group had three fingers, similar to those of birds.

Ornithopod fossils have been found worldwide—even in Antarctica! These animals first appeared in the Middle Jurassic period, reaching their maximum numbers in the Cretaceous period.

There were two main ancestries: the small, light hypsilophodonts and the more developed, large and heavy iguanodonts. The hypsilophodonts measured less than 6.5 feet long on average. They were two-legged and could run fast when attacked. The tails were long, with hardened connecting tissues to help them balance while running.

The iguanodonts included *Iguanodon bernissartensis* as well as its close cousins *Dryosaurus*, *Camptosaurus*, and *Talenkauen*.

Scientists now believe that *Iguanodon atherfieldensis* should be called *Mantellisaurus*, after Gideon Mantell, who discovered it.

OURANOSAURUS

This extraordinary-looking iguanodont lived in Africa in the Early Cretaceous Period. It had a large hump of fat on its back supported by neural spines.

Tall neural spines on back

Neural spines on tail

THE DISCOVERER
Iguanodon was only the second dinosaur to be given a scientific name (after *Megalosaurus*). It was discovered and named by the British scientist Gideon Mantell in the 1820s.

PHYLOGENETIC TREE

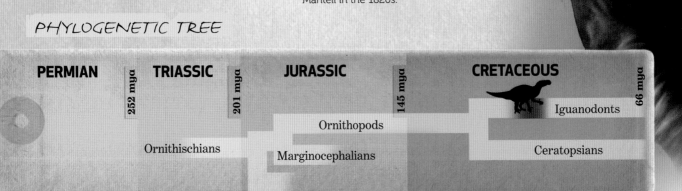

PERMIAN	252 mya	TRIASSIC	201 mya	JURASSIC	145 mya	CRETACEOUS	66 mya
							Iguanodonts
				Ornithopods			
Ornithischians			Marginocephalians				Ceratopsians

SKELETON
The hind legs were very strong to carry the whole weight of *Iguanodon* when it reared up.

SPIKED THUMB
The thumb of *Iguanodon* formed a big spike. When the fossil remains of *Iguanodon* were first assembled, the thumb spike was thought to have been a horn from its nose!

Iguanodon

IGUANA TEETH
Iguanodon's teeth were arranged in long rows at the sides of the mouth. Each one of them was similar to a modern iguana's tooth, but much larger.

HANDS
The hands were strong and rigid. The big spike on the thumb was used for defense, while the middle fingers supported the body weight. The outer finger was able to fold in toward the other fingers, much like a human thumb.

HIP
The front portion of the hip bones was directed backward. This position helped in the development of the digestive system by allowing more space for a large stomach and, therefore, more efficient digestion.

LEGS
Iguanodon moved mainly on all four limbs, although it could also stand on two legs if it needed to reach higher vegetation or fight off rivals and predators.

Carnivores

Theropod means "beast feet" and indicates that dinosaurs in this group had pointed claws at their toes. Theropods were carnivores, well suited to running and hunting efficiently.

Carnivorous dinosaurs are grouped within Theropoda, one of the main ancestries. Together with the herbivorous sauropodomorphs, Theropoda form the large group of saurischian dinosaurs. The earliest theropods appeared during the Late Triassic period, 230 million years ago. They already had features that included sharp, curved teeth, loose arms with cutting claws, hips adapted for fast movement, and long tails to help the animals balance themselves.

The oldest theropods, *Herrerasaurus* and *Eoraptor*, were discovered in Argentina. *Eoraptor* was around 3 feet in length, but *Herrerasaurus* was a bigger predator. In North America, more advanced theropods, such as *Coelophysis* and *Dilophosaurus,* emerged from these early forms. At the end of the Jurassic period, the first large theropods appeared —*Allosaurus,* for example, which reached up to 40 feet in length. Varied forms appeared during the Cretaceous period, from the very large *Giganotosaurus* to the pigeon-sized *Ligabueino.*

Tetanuran theropods included a wide range of forms, from gigantic predators to small-sized, insect-eating animals. Their evolution is still continuing today, because birds are examples of this group.

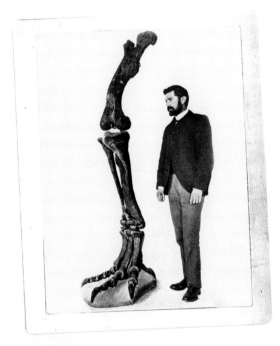

THEROPOD LEG
Paleontologist Othniel C. Marsh invented the term *Theropoda.* He discovered fossils of *Allosaurus* (whose leg appears in the photo) and *Ceratosaurus,* both from the Jurassic period.

BIG HUNTERS
Allosaurus lived at the end of the Jurassic period, around 146 million years ago. It fed on lizard-hipped and bird-hipped dinosaurs such as *Dryosaurus*.

SHORT AND LONG

Alvarezsaurus had very short arms that hardly extended from its body. It used them to dig into termite mounds in search of food. *Epidendrosaurus*, however, had very long fingers, which it used to catch insects from the bark of trees.

Alvarezsaurus

Epidendrosaurus

THEROPOD HIP
Theropod hip bones had large areas where big leg muscles were attached. This allowed them to run quickly in order to chase their prey.

Ceratosaurs

During the Jurassic period, the ceratosaurs (horned reptiles) and the tetanurans (stiff tails) were the two main ancestries of theropod dinosaurs. *Ceratosaurus* and *Carnotaurus*, from the Cretaceous period, are two examples of ceratosaurs.

During the Cretaceous period, the abelisaurs were the ceratosaurs that dominated Gondwana. *Carnotaurus* was the grandest of them all. It got its name from its flesh-eating habits and its horns, which were similar to those of a bull. Its skeleton was found in rocks in South America, but close relatives have also been found in India, Africa, and Madagascar. It had tiny forelimbs that were practically useless, but hind legs that were slender, sleek and well adapted for running. The skull was short and broad and attached to a very strong, wide neck. *Carnotaurus* was around 30 feet long and weighed over a ton.

THE DISCOVERER
The only skeleton of *Carnotaurus* was found in 1984 by an Argentinian paleontologist named José Bonaparte. It was embedded in a very hard kind of rock, so it was very difficult to dig out! Bonaparte described this new species in 1985 as *Carnotaurus sastrei*.

SKIN
Carnotaurus' skin was covered with scalelike bumps and wrinkles, probably for protection from attack.

MULTIPURPOSE FEET
Theropod feet were adapted to support the weight of the dinosaur, and to provide power for jumping and speed for running. They had three toes and sharp, pointed claws.

THEROPOD DIVERSITY
The separation of Laurasia and Gondwana in the Cretaceous period gave rise to different theropod forms in different regions: tyrannosaurs and ornithomimids in the north; carcharadontosaurs, abelisaurs, and unenlagids in the south.

Coelurus was 8 ft long.

Gallimimus was 20 ft long.

HORNS
Carnotaurus had strong outgrowths that pointed outward, similar to horns on a bull.

JAWS
Carnotaurus had many sharp teeth.

Ekrixinatosaurus was a relative of *Carnotaurus* and was 36 feet long.

Daspletosaurus was part of the tyrannosaurid family and was 30 feet long.

Tyrannotitan was a relative of *Giganotosaurus* and was 40 feet long.

Giganotosaurus

As its name suggests, *Giganotosaurus* was a gigantic dinosaur, one of the biggest carnivorous dinosaurs ever to have existed! It lived in South America around 90 million years ago.

This "giant southern reptile" was an enormous predator. It was 44 feet long, and its skull measured 6 feet! It had a large mouth with teeth so sharp that one bite easily slashed through the flesh and muscles of its prey.

Giganotosaurus had extremely strong bones, particularly in its hind legs, which were thicker and wider than those of an African elephant. Its huge body weight and the size of its legs indicate that this animal had a slow and heavy walk, so it could not have run to hunt its prey. However, as it preyed upon titanosaurs, who couldn't run fast either, this was not a disadvantage.

Giganotosaurus belongs to a group of huge theropod dinosaurs known as the carcharodontosaurids, which included perhaps the largest land predators ever known. The group includes *Carcharodontosaurus* itself, *Tyrannotitan*, and *Mapusaurus*.

GENUS: GIGANOTOSAURUS
CLASSIFICATION: THEROPODA, TETANURAE, CARNOSAURIA

LENGTH 44 ft
WEIGHT 18,000 lb
DIET Carnivorous

HUGE SKULL
The skull of *Giganotosaurus* was one of the largest among the theropods. Compared with the rest of the body, the head was supersized.

LOCATION
Giganotosaurus and its relatives *Tyrannotitan* and *Mapusaurus* were found in Cretaceous period rocks in Patagonia, Argentina.

Carcharodontosaurus was found in Egypt, and *Concavenator*, a smaller relative, was found in Spain.

Giganotosaurus

Concavenator, the oldest known carcharodontosaur, was found in Spain in rocks that were 130 million years old. This specimen was about 20 feet long, but some of its later relatives were bigger.

The name *Carcharodontosaurus* means "shark-toothed reptile," because these dinosaurs had very sharp teeth, similar to those of a shark. They had around 70 teeth to allow them to cut through meat, although the teeth were probably not strong enough to crunch bones.

Giganotosaurus and the carcharodontosaurs were some of the main carnivores populating Gondwana between 125 and 90 million years ago. But their numbers decreased, leading to their complete disappearance several million years before the massive extinction at the end of the Cretaceous period. The disappearance of the carcharodontosaurs, 90 million years ago, is still a mystery!

TEETH
Giganotosaurus had short, thin teeth, suitable for slicing through flesh!

THE DISCOVERER
An amateur fossil hunter called Rubén Carolini discovered *Giganotosaurus carolinii* in 1993. The fossil was described by the Argentinian paleontologists Rodolfo Coria and Leonardo Salgado, who named it after its discoverer.

PHYLOGENETIC TREE

PERMIAN	252 mya	TRIASSIC	201 mya	JURASSIC	145 mya	CRETACEOUS	66 mya
						Carnosaurs	
		Theropods				Coelurosaurs	

SMELL
It is believed that *Giganotosaurus*'s sense of smell was more developed than its sight, as smell was very helpful for detecting its prey.

THE LARGEST PREDATORS

Giganotosaurus was bigger and heavier than *Tyrannosaurus rex*. But *Spinosaurus*, found in Africa, was the largest land predator, reaching up to 60 feet in length!

PREY
Giganotosaurus could knock down large herbivorous dinosaurs, such as titanosaurs.

BALANCING ACT
The tail balanced the body when the animal moved.

Giganotosaurus

ARMS
It is believed that *Giganotosaurus* had short but strong arms, with three clawed fingers.

SKULL
Giganotosaurus had large cavities near its eyes that helped to reduce the weight of its huge skull.

HEAVY LEGS
Giganotosaurus walked on its huge, powerful back legs, which were supported by the central toes of its feet.

POWERFUL TAIL
The tail had many bones and powerful muscles in order to balance the body. This allowed *Giganotosaurus* to turn its body quickly and attack suddenly.

Deinonychus

FEATHERS
The tip of the tail was covered with feathers, but it is not known whether it had the wide range of feathers that have been found in *Microraptor* and *Caudipteryx*.

Deinonychus relied on its lethal, sickle-shaped claws for attack and defense. Its name actually means "terrible claw"!

In 1964, the American paleontologist John Ostrom and his team discovered around 1,000 *Deinonychus* bones at a site in the western United States. The specimens included many well-preserved parts, including skulls. Ostrom also found a large number of eggshells underneath adult bones. This indicated that *Deinonychus* provided warmth for its eggs by sitting on them, in the same way that present-day birds hatch their eggs.

Deinonychus lived in hot, humid forests with other carnivores, including the large theropod *Acrocanthosaurus*, the ankylosaur *Sauropelta*, the ornithopod *Tenontosaurus*, and the enormous sauropod *Sauroposeidon*. *Deinonychus* is one of the best-known members of the dromaeosauridae family, which also includes dinosaurs such as *Microraptor*, *Unenlagia*, and *Utahraptor*.

GENUS: DEINONYCHUS
CLASSIFICATION: THEROPODA, COELUROSAURIA, DEINONYCHOSAURIA

LENGTH 11.5 ft
WEIGHT 176 lb
DIET Carnivorous

LINHERAPTOR SKELETON
This almost complete skeleton of *Linheraptor*, a close relative of *Deinonychus*, was found in Mongolia.

HUNTER'S ARMS
Deinonychus's arms folded at the sides of the body but could quickly stretch out to capture prey.

LOCATION
In the United States, *Deinonychus* fossils have been found in rocks that are 110 million years old.

In Asia, many deinonychosaurs, including *Microraptor*, *Velociraptor*, and *Linheraptor*, have been found.

Deinonychus

The dromaeosaurids appeared in the middle of the Jurassic period and disappeared at the end of the Cretaceous period. *Velociraptor* was the first to be discovered by paleontologists in 1923, in the Gobi Desert, Mongolia. Since then, feathered dinosaurs such as *Sinornithosaurus millenii* have been found in other places, particularly in China.

The dromaeosaurids are thought to be closely related to the troodontids, theropods that also had a sickle-shaped claw on each foot. Because of this strange weapon that they had in common, dromaeosaurids and troodontids are grouped together as *deinonychosaurs*, which means "fearsome claw reptiles."

It was Ostrom who first drew attention to the noticeable similarities between *Deinonychus* and *Archaeopteryx*, the oldest known bird. He changed the way paleontologists thought about dinosaurs, suggesting that they had far more in common with big, flightless birds (such as ostriches) than with reptiles.

BLADE TEETH
Deinonychus had powerful jaws, with around 70 curved, bladelike teeth.

THE DISCOVERER
The North American paleontologist John Ostrom, pictured with a reconstructed skeleton of *Deinonychus*. His theories about the links between dinosaurs and birds caused great controversy among paleontologists, and sparked new research into the evolution of birds.

PHYLOGENETIC TREE

PERMIAN	252 mya	TRIASSIC	201 mya	JURASSIC	145 mya	CRETACEOUS	99 mya

 Dromaeosaurids

Maniraptors

Birds

Coelurosaurs

Oviraptorosaurs

SKELETON
The thorax was short and upright, similar to the thorax in birds. The neck curved upward, holding the head in a high position.

CLAWED FEET
The claw on the second toe was up to 5 inches long and very sharp!

Deinonychus

SKULL
Deinonychus had strong jaws, with many small, sharp teeth. The snout was narrow, and its bite was very powerful.

TAIL
The bones at the tip of the tail were connected by long, hardened tissues, making it very strong. This helped *Deinonychus* to maintain its balance.

HANDS
Deinonychus had large hands with three long fingers ending in curved claws. These were helpful for grasping and tearing prey.

SHARP VISION
The structure of the bones in the skull allowed both eyes to face forward, which gave *Deinonychus* good 3-D vision.

HUNTING IN PACKS
Several skeletons of *Deinonychus* and of the ornithopod *Tenontosaurus* were found together in the United States. This suggests that they hunted in groups or gathered together to feed.

Attack and Defense

Dinosaurs developed a wide range of adaptations to suit their lifestyles. Carnivores developed speed and strength for attack, while herbivores developed different defensive strategies and gained body armor.

The carnivorous dinosaurs used their fast pace to hunt successfully. First, they detected prey through the senses of sight, smell, or hearing. Then, they used their strength to attack after a short-distance chase. They inflicted injuries in the most delicate parts of the body, such as the neck, then waited for the prey to bleed to death! It is likely that theropods hunted alone; however, it has been suggested that *Velociraptor* and *Deinonychus* hunted in packs.

Herbivorous dinosaurs developed a variety of strategies to defend themselves. The small hypsilophodonts had long, slim legs so that they could run quickly. Iguanodonts had a very sharp spike on their hands to use as a weapon. Ankylosaurs and stegosaurs had body armor for protection. Ceratopsians (such as *Triceratops*) had pointed horns to fight with carnivores, and the big sauropods had long, thin tails that worked like whips. Herbivores also gathered together in herds for protection in numbers.

ANKYLOSAURUS VS. TYRANNOSAURUS REX

It would not have been easy for *Tyrannosaurus rex* to defeat *Ankylosaurus* because of *Ankylosaurus*'s armored body covering.

ARMOR
Ankylosaurus had thick armor on its back in the form of spikes, and a heavy club on the end of its tail.

BONY PLATES
Ankylosaurus's armor was made up of plates of bone known as osteoderms.

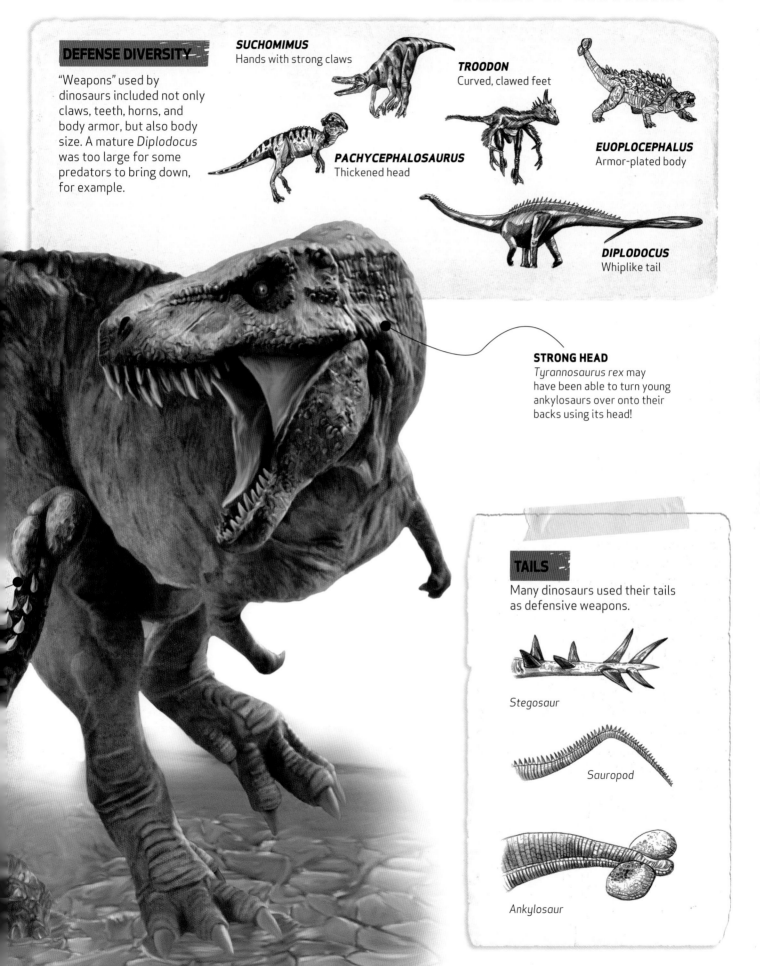

DEFENSE DIVERSITY

"Weapons" used by dinosaurs included not only claws, teeth, horns, and body armor, but also body size. A mature *Diplodocus* was too large for some predators to bring down, for example.

SUCHOMIMUS
Hands with strong claws

TROODON
Curved, clawed feet

PACHYCEPHALOSAURUS
Thickened head

EUOPLOCEPHALUS
Armor-plated body

DIPLODOCUS
Whiplike tail

STRONG HEAD
Tyrannosaurus rex may have been able to turn young ankylosaurs over onto their backs using its head!

TAILS

Many dinosaurs used their tails as defensive weapons.

Stegosaur

Sauropod

Ankylosaur

Dinosaur Battle

Protoceratopsians evolved into ceratopsians such as *Triceratops*. They had horns and crests of different sizes and shapes on their skulls that they used to defend themselves against predators. Together with the hadrosaur *Edmontosaurus*, the ceratopsians formed the largest herbivorous herds in America.

One of the most famous skeletons of *Protoceratops* was found intertwined with a *Velociraptor* fossil. A group of paleontologists discovered these skeletons in 1971, in Mongolia. The two dinosaurs must have been fighting. One foot of *Velociraptor* is pointing its sickle-shaped claw into a delicate area of *Protoceratops*'s neck! It is thought that both animals died together when they were suddenly buried by a sandstorm 70 million years ago.

SIZE
Protoceratops walked on four legs and was the size of a present-day African elephant.

HERBIVOROUS THEROPODS
Therizinosaurs were strange theropods that evolved from meat-eating ancestors into herbivores. They developed enormous claws, which, in addition to being used for collecting food, would have been useful in defense.

SHARP CLAWS
Velociraptor grasped its prey with its sharp claws. The foot also ended in a long claw, like a razor-sharp hook.

SPEED
Both carnivorous and herbivorous dinosaurs developed light, long legs, similar to those of flightless birds like the ostrich. This helped them to run fast when chasing prey or escaping from predators.

HUMAN

DROMICEIOMIMUS

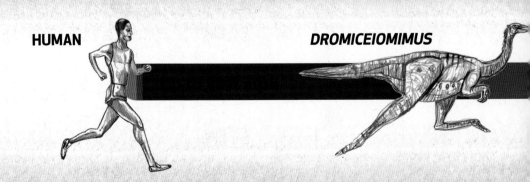

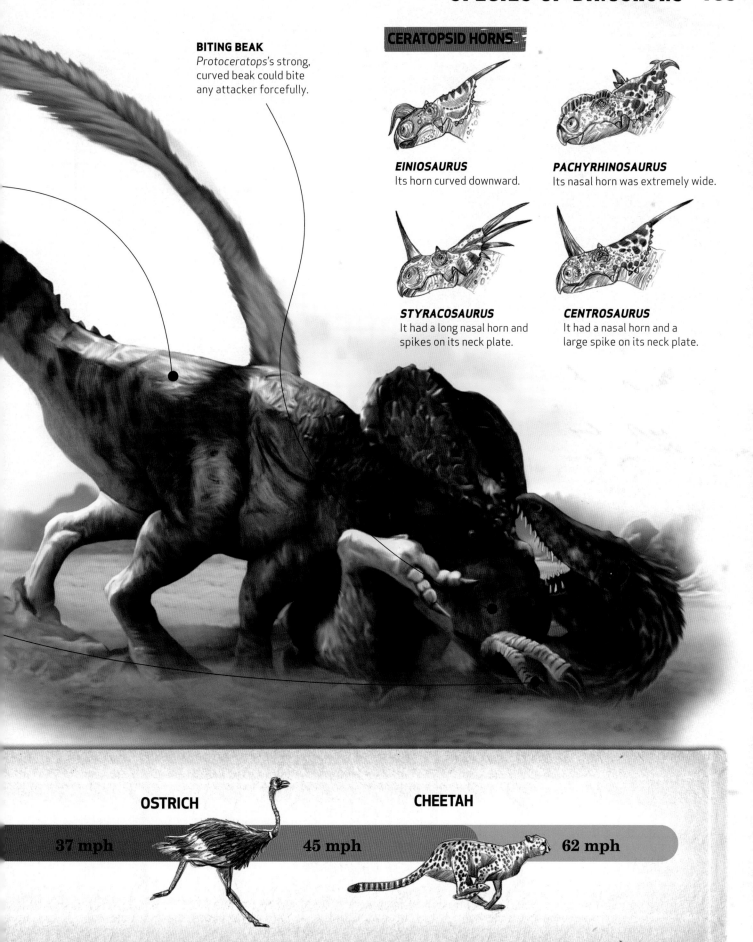

BITING BEAK
Protoceratops's strong, curved beak could bite any attacker forcefully.

CERATOPSID HORNS

EINIOSAURUS
Its horn curved downward.

PACHYRHINOSAURUS
Its nasal horn was extremely wide.

STYRACOSAURUS
It had a long nasal horn and spikes on its neck plate.

CENTROSAURUS
It had a nasal horn and a large spike on its neck plate.

OSTRICH

CHEETAH

37 mph   45 mph   62 mph

Triceratops

Triceratops horridus (three-horned face) lived in North America during the last 3 million years of the Mesozoic Era.

Triceratops was described for the first time in 1889, and since then hundreds of examples have been found, including specimens of both young and mature animals. This herbivore had a huge skull, around 8 feet long, and reached 30 feet in length and 10 feet in height. It is believed that the largest animals may have weighed 12 tons! *Triceratops* was a four-legged dinosaur that could not raise itself up on its hind legs. It fed on low, tough plants that it cut with its powerful beak. The front limbs had three fingers, while the back legs had four toes, all of them with rounded hooves.

Triceratops had a short horn above the nostrils and two long horns above its eyes. Underneath, the long horns were part of the bone structure of the skull, but the bone was covered by the horn material. Just like present-day bulls, buffaloes, and antelopes, the horns regrew if they wore out or broke off.

GENUS: TRICERATOPS
CLASSIFICATION: ORNITHISCHIA,
MARGINOCEPHALIA, CERATOPSIA

LENGTH 30 ft
WEIGHT 26,500 lb
DIET Herbivorous

NECK PLATE
The rear part of the skull pointed backward, to form a protective neck covering.

BEAK JAWS
Triceratops had powerful jaws that were tipped with a pointed beak.

LOCATION
Triceratops has been found in North America. It is unknown in other parts of the world.

Distant relatives of *Triceratops* have been found in Asia, most of them without horns.

Triceratops

Like all ceratopsians, *Triceratops* had a large outgrowth of bones at the back of the skull that protected the soft neck area. Research suggests that it used its horns as defensive weapons against predators, such as *Tyrannosaurus rex*. However, in dinosaurs such as *Styracosaurus* the horns were only about an inch thick, so they wouldn't have been strong enough for this.

Skulls have been found of both young and adult *Triceratops*. The young animals had already developed horns and neck frills. In the older *Triceratops* the horns had grown in length and thickness. The bony neck plate grew backward and became thinner.

Both the horns and the neck plates may have helped *Triceratops* parents to recognize their offspring, as each dinosaur would have had small differences in the size and shape of their horns and neck frills. They may also have been used to show dominance among other *Triceratops*, and to help find a mate.

HORN EVOLUTION

Ceratopsians evolved from having very small horns and neck frills, like *Leptoceratops*, to having larger and more varied forms, such as *Pentasaurus*.

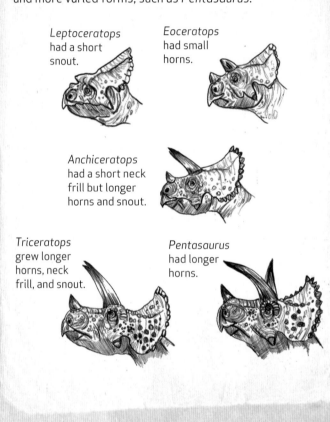

Leptoceratops had a short snout.

Eoceratops had small horns.

Anchiceratops had a short neck frill but longer horns and snout.

Triceratops grew longer horns, neck frill, and snout.

Pentasaurus had longer horns.

PHYLOGENETIC TREE

PERMIAN	252 mya	TRIASSIC	201 mya	JURASSIC	145 mya	CRETACEOUS	66 mya
						Ceratopsians	
				Marginocephalians			
Ornithischians							

SKELETON
You can see the neck plate is part of the skull in this reconstruction of the skeleton of *Triceratops horridus*.

POSTURE
Paleontologists originally thought that *Triceratops*'s front legs pointed in an outward direction, similar to present-day reptiles, Today, we know that they had a straighter posture, as shown in the lower picture.

Triceratops

THREE-HORNED FACE
The name *Triceratops* means "three-horned face." In addition to these horns, *Triceratops* had many small spikes along the edge of its neck frill.

TEETH
Triceratops's teeth were arranged in groups, called batteries. The largest animals could have had up to 800 teeth!

FEET
The feet ended in rounded hooves with four short toes.

TAIL
The tail was short. It was not needed to balance the body, as it did for *Triceratops*'s two-footed ancestors.

FRONT LEGS
The powerful front legs supported the weight at the front of the body and provided extra strength when attacking enemies.

Warm- or Cold-Blooded?

Scientists share the view that dinosaurs had more advanced behavior, skills, and adaptations than present-day reptiles. It is now thought that, due to their many similarities with birds, dinosaurs were warm-blooded instead of cold-blooded.

DINOSAUR HERESIES
Robert Bakker studied with John Ostrom in the 1960s and strongly supported the view that dinosaurs were warm-blooded animals. His book *The Dinosaur Heresies* presented these new ideas to the general public and caused great controversy when it was published in 1986.

For a long time, paleontologists believed dinosaurs were slow-moving, cold-blooded animals. But new research carried out by John Ostrom challenged these views.

Along with Ostrom, American paleontologist Robert Bakker supported the view that dinosaurs were warm-blooded animals, similar to birds and mammals. Bakker argued that the position of dinosaurs' legs straight underneath their bodies, and their ability to move fast with long steps, provided evidence to support this. He showed that they had hair and feathers, similar to warm-blooded birds and mammals, which would have helped to preserve heat in the body. This further supported the idea that many dinosaurs were warm-blooded animals.

COLD OR WARM

In cold-blooded animals, such as toads, the body temperature varies according to the surrounding air temperature. In warm-blooded animals, such as hamsters, body temperature remains roughly constant and is controlled internally by the body.

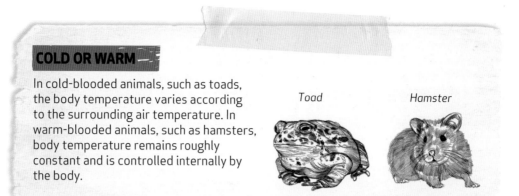

Toad

Hamster

FEATHER COVERINGS
Many dinosaurs, including *Psittacosaurus*, were covered in feathers.

BEAK
Psittacosaurus had a powerful beak on its upper jaw.

FAST RUNNER
Psittacosaurus could walk on two or four legs. It may have been a fast runner, which would have helped this dinosaur escape predators.

Diet and Environment

Cold-blooded carnivores only need to consume small amounts of food. However, warm-blooded predators, such as lions, need a larger amount of food for energy and to maintain body temperature.

Some paleontologists doubted whether herbivorous dinosaurs could be warm-blooded. They thought that slow-growing Mesozoic plants, such as conifers, cycads, ginkgos, and ferns, would not have been enough to sustain these dinosaurs. However, in various experiments, ginkgos were grown in atmospheric conditions identical to the climate of the Mesozoic era. It was found that the ginkgos grew better and had far more nutrients (substances needed for growth) than they do in today's conditions! Therefore, it's likely that conditions in the time of the dinosaurs would have allowed even warm-blooded herbivores to get enough food necessary for living.

FIRST DISCOVERIES
The first sign that there was such a thing as polar dinosaurs came in 1960, when dinosaur footprints were found at Spitsbergen, an island between the coast of Norway and the North Pole.

POLAR DINOSAURS
In 2009, fossil hunters in northeastern Russia discovered the remains of duck-billed dinosaurs, teeth belonging to relatives of *Triceratops*, and even tyrannosaurid teeth! This area would have been inside the Arctic Circle when the dinosaurs were alive, with temperatures as low as 50 degrees Fahrenheit.

LIVING FOSSILS
Ginkgos are nonflowering plants that date back around 270 million years. Ginkgo fossils have been found in many parts of the world. These plants still grow today.

DARKNESS
Polar dinosaurs may have had to
endure prolonged darkness for
up to six months each winter.

FEATHERS
Feathers may have helped
polar dinosaurs to retain
body heat in order to
survive in cold climates.

Argentinosaurus

Argentinosaurus is the largest dinosaur we know existed. The study of this giant has helped us to learn more about enormous plant-eating sauropods.

Argentinosaurus *huinculensis* was named in 1993 after the Huincul Formation in southwest Argentina, where paleontologists recovered its fossil in 1989. Its scientific name means "Argentinean lizard." Only parts of the skeleton were recovered, including some vertebrae, ribs, a shinbone, and thigh bone.

When it was first discovered, *Argentinosaurus* attracted international attention because of its size. Sauropods of similar sizes include *Paralititan, Supersaurus, Seismosaurus, Sauroposeidon, Alamosaurus*, and *Puertasaurus*.

In 2014, a possible *Argentinosaurus* fossil was discovered near Trelew, Argentina. At 130 feet long and weighing 85 tons, this dinosaur could be the largest ever discovered!

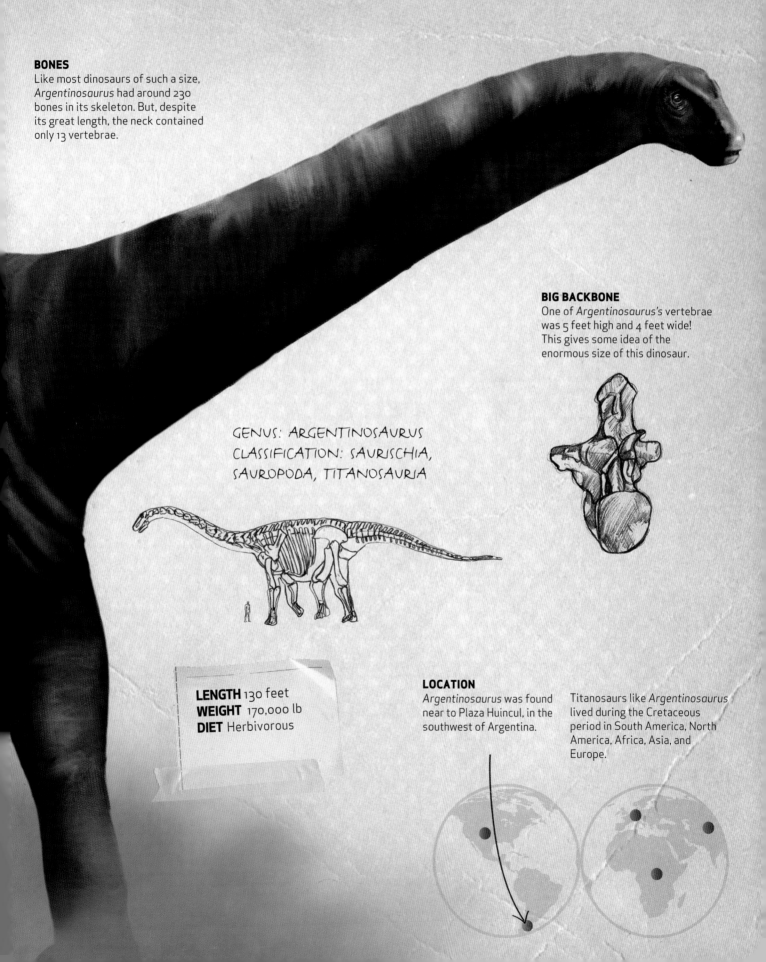

BONES

Like most dinosaurs of such a size, *Argentinosaurus* had around 230 bones in its skeleton. But, despite its great length, the neck contained only 13 vertebrae.

BIG BACKBONE

One of *Argentinosaurus*'s vertebrae was 5 feet high and 4 feet wide! This gives some idea of the enormous size of this dinosaur.

GENUS: ARGENTINOSAURUS
CLASSIFICATION: SAURISCHIA, SAUROPODA, TITANOSAURIA

LENGTH 130 feet
WEIGHT 170,000 lb
DIET Herbivorous

LOCATION

Argentinosaurus was found near to Plaza Huincul, in the southwest of Argentina.

Titanosaurs like *Argentinosaurus* lived during the Cretaceous period in South America, North America, Africa, Asia, and Europe.

Argentinosaurus

The reason for the giant size of *Argentinosaurus* and other sauropods remains a mystery. One explanation may be the increase in temperatures during the Mesozoic era, as present-day reptiles living near the equator tend to be larger than those in colder regions. It could also have been the result of feeding on plants that were low in nutrients. In order to digest them, sauropods would have needed to keep the vegetation in their stomachs and intestines for a long time. As they evolved, their bodies may have gotten bigger to fit their enlarged stomachs.

COMPARING NEIGHBORS

Of the nearly 60 species of sauropods, theropods, and ornithischians found in Argentina, *Argentinosaurus* is one of the most famous. Its size makes it stand out among the dinosaurs.

Argentinosaurus

PHYLOGENETIC TREE

PERMIAN	252 mya	TRIASSIC	201 mya	JURASSIC	145 mya	CRETACEOUS	66 mya

Sauropods

Titanosaurs

THE RESEARCHERS
José Bonaparte and Rodolfo Coria wrote the scientific description and gave *Argentinosaurus* its name in 1993. The original fossils form part of the collections of the Carmen Funes Museum in Plaza Huincul.

THE DISCOVERER
Rancher Guillermo Heredia found the remains of *Argentinosaurus* in 1989, while staying in Plaza Huincul. He immediately informed the local museum of paleontology and helped to recover the fossil. Four years later, the actual value of his discovery would be known to all!

Argentinosaurus

LONG LEGS
Only a few bones have been found, including a fibula (lower leg) and a femur (thigh). The fibula was 5 feet long and the femur would have reached up to 8 feet.

TAIL
The tail was not as long as in other sauropods. It was very flexible and had more than 30 bones. Its flexibility may have meant that *Argentinosaurus* could rear up on its hind legs better than some of its sauropod relatives.

WEIGHT SAVING
In order to reduce the weight of the skeleton, the inner tissue of the spinal bone was spongy and had huge cavities, surrounded by very thin walls.

SKELETON
Scientists use comparisons with other more complete skeletons of similar dinosaurs to estimate *Argentinosaurus's* true size. *Argentinosaurus* may have been as long as three buses end to end.

Finding Food

Dinosaurs developed varied adaptations in order to find food. The shape of their teeth, their stomach contents, and their fossilized feces all tell us about the kind of food they ate.

DRAGONFLY
Fossils show that insects such as dragonflies were present on the planet much earlier than dinosaurs. They were the main source of food for small flesh-eating animals, because they were plentiful and readily available.

The earliest dinosaurs appeared in small forms, some as small as chickens. These dinosaurs had tiny, pointed teeth and fed mainly on insects and other invertebrates they found among plant leaves.

As the descendants of these dinosaurs grew bigger, they started to hunt larger animals. *Eoraptor* was the size of a turkey and may have fed on reptiles the size of lizards. *Herrerasaurus* reached 20 feet in length, and ate prey the size of wild boars.

In the Triassic period, other small dinosaurs appeared that fed on a diet of insects, but later they replaced them with plants.

At the same time, the first gigantic (sauropodomorph) and bird-hipped (ornithischian) dinosaurs made their appearance. The sauropodomorphs soon reached the size of giraffes. Their necks increased in length, and they were able to get closer to high treetops to pull off leaves, branches, and fruits. Ornithischians developed a beak and a complex set of teeth to help them grind their food.

VELOCIRAPTOR THE HUNTER
Velociraptor fought with larger animals, such as *Protoceratops*. It killed them with its curved claws and large, sharp teeth.

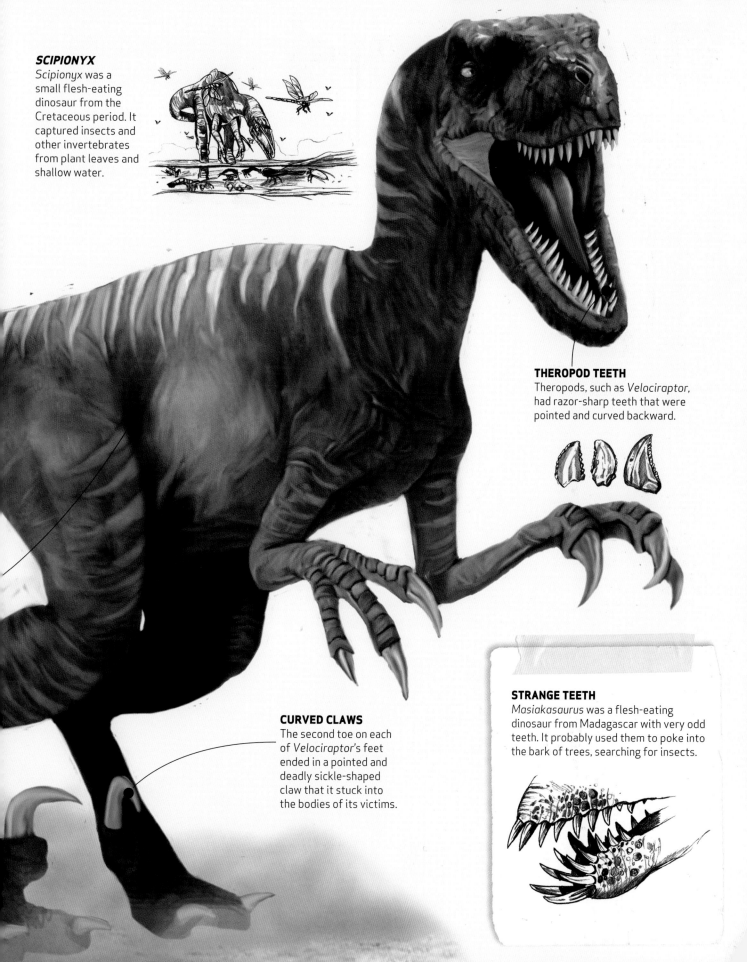

SCIPIONYX
Scipionyx was a small flesh-eating dinosaur from the Cretaceous period. It captured insects and other invertebrates from plant leaves and shallow water.

THEROPOD TEETH
Theropods, such as *Velociraptor*, had razor-sharp teeth that were pointed and curved backward.

CURVED CLAWS
The second toe on each of *Velociraptor*'s feet ended in a pointed and deadly sickle-shaped claw that it stuck into the bodies of its victims.

STRANGE TEETH
Masiakasaurus was a flesh-eating dinosaur from Madagascar with very odd teeth. It probably used them to poke into the bark of trees, searching for insects.

Therizinosaurus

Therizinosaurus had a strong body, with long arms and two legs. There was doubt about its classification for years, because of its odd appearance. New finds of complete skeletons show that therizinosaurs were herbivorous theropods.

During the 1940s, paleontologists from the USSR and Mongolia working together in the Gobi Desert discovered some very strange fossils. They were the front limbs of a reptile with amazingly long claws. For decades, the appearance of this animal and its relationship with other dinosaurs remained a mystery. However, the specimens were so large and interesting that eventually the appearance of this mysterious beast was reconstructed.

At first, the remains confused researchers when they tried to classify them. Russian paleontologist Evgeny Maleev thought that they belonged to a turtle-like reptile. He gave it the name *Therizinosaurus* (scythe lizard). However, new samples found in 1950 helped paleontologists to recognize it as a dinosaur. Several decades after its first discovery, it was classified as a theropod.

GENUS: THERIZINOSAURUS
CLASSIFICATION: SAURISCHIA, THEROPODA, THERIZINOSAURIDAE

LENGTH 33 ft
WEIGHT 11,000 lb
DIET Herbivorous

STURDY ARM
Each arm had a powerful muscle system, which continued up to the shoulder.

LOCATION
Remains of *Therizinosaurus* came from various rock formations in the region of the Gobi Desert, in Mongolia and China.

PLANT DIET
Therizinosaurus had a plant-based diet, even though it belonged to the same group as carnivorous dinosaurs such as *Velociraptor*.

STRANGE FEATURES
Despite being classified as a theropod, *Therizinosaurus* had a bird's hip, like the ornithischians, and four toes on each leg.

Therizinosaurus

Although the known remains of *Therizinosaurus* are incomplete, it has been possible to do a reconstruction of its entire body from studies that compare it with other dinosaurs. It probably had a strong body, with a long neck ending in a small skull. Like the earliest bird-hipped dinosaurs, it moved on two legs, each ending in four toes. This was different from other theropods, which had only three toes.

Therizinosaurus's arms were up to 8 feet long with three digits and an enormous claw on each one. It is possible the claws were up to 3 feet in length! Some paleontologists believe they were used as weapons for defense, or in fights for territory. We also know now that *Therizinosaurus* was herbivorous, so it could have used its claws as a tool to cut the branches of trees, as present-day sloths do.

Some *Therizinosaurus* bones were discovered near fossilized eggs in 2013. These may have been from parents who took care of their eggs.

FIRST FINDINGS
Fossils of *Therizinosaurus* were discovered in 1948, in the Nemegt Formation of the Gobi Desert (see pages 64-65), in the southwest of Mongolia.

CLOSE RELATIVES

Together with other species such as *Beipiaosaurus*, *Nothronychus*, and *Alxasaurus*, *Therizinosaurus* formed a group that was defined only in the 1990s.

Alxasaurus   Nothronychus

Beipiaosaurus

PHYLOGENETIC TREE

PERMIAN	252 mya	TRIASSIC	201 mya	JURASSIC	145 mya	CRETACEOUS	66 mya

Theropods

Coelurosaurs

Therizinosaurs

CLAWS

The largest of *Therizinosaurus*'s three claws was on the first digit. These claws may have been used to cut leaves, branches, and other vegetation.

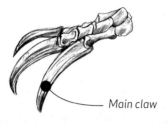

Main claw

BROAD BODY

Therizinosaurus had a wide pelvis, which probably meant it had a broad, deep body similar to that of present-day ostriches.

DEADLY ATTACK

Therizinosaurus was probably prey for *Tarbosaurus*. Even its amazing claws would have been little help against the attack of this fierce dinosaur.

Therizinosaurus

LONG AND SHORT
We know the amazing length of *Therizinosaurus*'s arms from the discovery of a complete set of fossil bones. Its legs and tail, however, were short compared to its arms.

SKELETON
The fossil remains of *Therizinosaurus* are incomplete. In order to reconstruct it, paleontologists have studied dinosaurs such as *Erlikosaurus* and *Segnosaurus*.

SKULL
No fossil skull has been discovered for *Therizinosaurus*, so reconstruction of the head is based on paleontologists' knowledge of similar dinosaurs.

CLAWS
Therizinosaurus's sharp claws are the longest known claws in an animal.

HIP STRUCTURE
Therizinosaurus had a hip structure similar to that of modern-day birds. It is possible that this shape helped to accommodate its long intestines.

Dinosaur Families

Along with teeth, skeletons, and footprints, a variety of fossilized dinosaur eggs, nests, and embryos have been found. They have given us some surprising information about the early life of these animals.

Fossil remains show us that many dinosaurs nested in colonies. The eggs that have been found are of many different shapes and sizes.

Just as with present-day reptiles, the eggs had a protective shell. The tough outer shell explains how thousands of dinosaur eggs have been preserved as fossils.

The eggs were either covered by plants or incubated (kept warm so that they could develop) by the dinosaur parents. Parents may also have sat on their eggs in order to protect them from predators. We have learned a lot of information from discoveries of nests, with unhatched eggs and baby skeletons, belonging to the hadrosaur *Maiasaura*.

Baby *Maiasaura* dinosaurs would have fit in the palm of a human hand! Their parents protected them and taught them where to go for food and water.

It is likely that dinosaurs could make sounds as signals to their young, just as birds do today, to create strong parental bonds.

EGGS

The shape, size, and color of eggs varied according to the group of dinosaur.

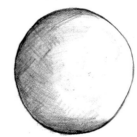

Chicken

Velociraptor

Hypselosaurus

Oviraptor

Neuquensaurus

HATCHING

The eggs of *Oviraptor* were almost 6 inches long! This reconstruction of an embryo that is about to hatch is based on the findings of hundreds of eggs in Cretaceous rocks from the Gobi Desert, Mongolia.

Oviraptor *embryo*

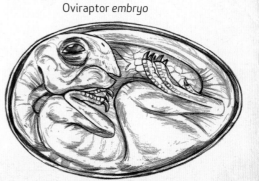

BEAK
Maiasaura's wide beak helped it to transport large quantities of food to the nest.

PROTECTIVE PARENTS
After being born, the young remained in the nest, where adults fed them.

Early Care

Oviraptor and *Velociraptor* dinosaurs incubated their young by sitting on top of their nests and controlling the temperature of the eggs directly with their own bodies. The first proof of this behavior was seen in *Oviraptor* fossils in the Gobi Desert. The skeletons were found on top of their eggs, with their legs in the center of the litter and their arms extended over the edges.

Skeleton of an *Oviraptor* sitting on its eggs and providing warmth for them.

PROTOCERATOPS

Protoceratops was an ancient relative of *Triceratops*. Many specimens were discovered in Mongolia, which indicated they lived in herds. The young of this herbivore measured 7 inches, while the adults reached 6.5 feet in length.

Parents took care of the newborn babies.

The nest consisted of a circular hollow in the sand.

SNAKE THREAT

In India, the skeleton of a snake was found wrapped around a titanosaur nest! The snake could not have swallowed eggs, but it could have swallowed newborn babies.

THE ARMS
Oviraptor had feathered arms that helped to maintain the temperature of the eggs.

FEEDING THEIR YOUNG

A mother *Oviraptor* is shown regurgitating (bringing up) swallowed food to give to one of her young. Regurgitation helped to process and soften the food for the young to eat.

Dinosaur eggs

Snake

Corythosaurus

Corythosaurus lived in large flocks in present-day Canada. It was a hadrosaur, or "duck-billed" dinosaur, and its remains were found in rocks over 76 million years old.

Paleontologist Barnum Brown gave *Corythosaurus* its name because its crest looked like the helmet of a Corinthian (ancient Greek) soldier! The North American paleontologist found the first skeleton of *Corythosaurus* in western Canada. The skeleton that was uncovered was nearly complete; some fossilized skin was even preserved on one side.

Hadrosaurs formed the most successful herbivorous group at the end of the Cretaceous period, mainly in North America and Asia, although fossils have been found in many parts of the world. Hadrosaurs had long snouts, rather like ducks' bills. Along their jaws were large numbers of teeth grouped in batteries, which they used to crush and grind vegetation. The most ancient hadrosaurs were the size of horses, but their descendants from the late Cretaceous period grew to up to 33 feet in length!

We know about the hadrosaurs' diet from skeletons with preserved, fossilized plant remains in the stomach area. There are also fossilized feces, which show that they ate leaves, fruits, and seeds.

LENGTH 33 ft
WEIGHT 9,000 lb
DIET Herbivorous

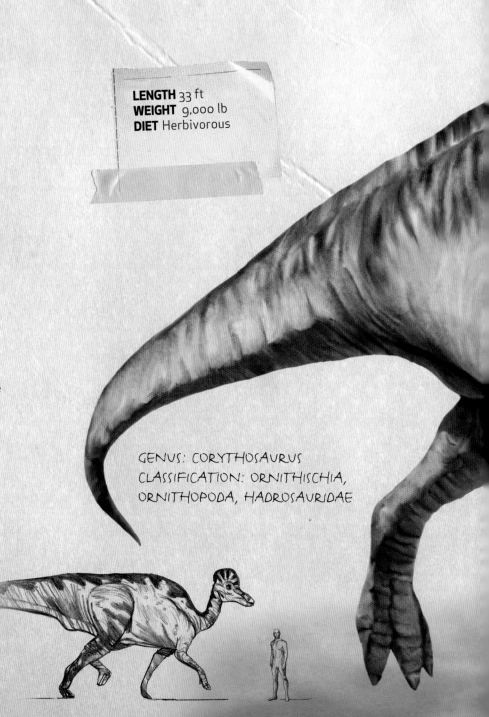

GENUS: CORYTHOSAURUS
CLASSIFICATION: ORNITHISCHIA, ORNITHOPODA, HADROSAURIDAE

CRESTS
The many species of hadrosaur can be recognized by the different structures of their crests.

THE DISCOVERER
In 1910, the American fossil hunter Barnum Brown led several successful expeditions in western Canada. There, the expeditions found a large variety of crest-headed hadrosaurs.

DIET
Corythosaurus raised itself up on its hind legs to eat leaves and fruits from conifers. It also ate ferns that it pulled out of the ground while walking on all four legs.

LOCATION
Hadrosaurs lived in large numbers in North America, but *Corythosaurus* has been found only in Canada.

Asia was home to many different hadrosaurs. Among them was the lambeosaurine (hadrosaurs with crests) *Aralosaurus*.

Corythosaurus

The skull of *Corythosaurus* was notable not only for the long snout, but also for the large nose! The nostrils were lined with tissues that produced moisture and helped to trap particles from the air while *Corythosaurus* was breathing.

The hadrosaurs are divided into two families; those with hollow crests, such as *Corythosaurus*, are known as lambeosaurines. In the lambeosaurines, the nasal passages extended into the crests on the top of the head. Paleontologists believe that by blowing air through the hollow passages in these crests, lambeosaurines could make loud sounds that would have carried over large distances. They probably helped to keep the lambeosaurines together and to send signals to warn off predators.

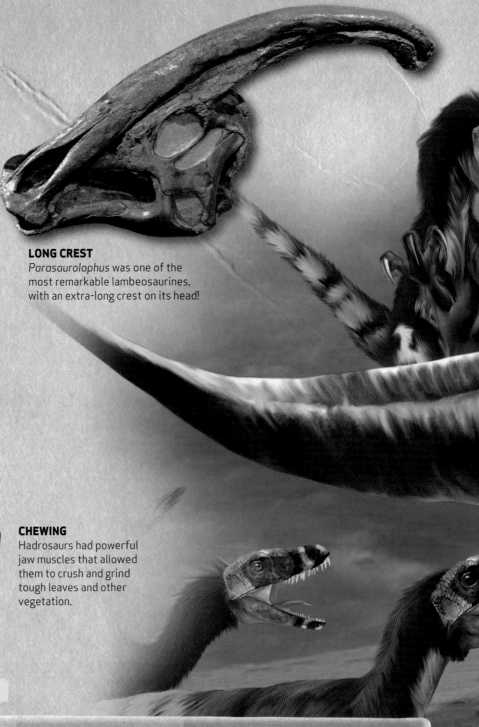

LONG CREST
Parasaurolophus was one of the most remarkable lambeosaurines, with an extra-long crest on its head!

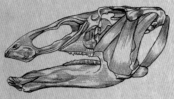

CHEWING
Hadrosaurs had powerful jaw muscles that allowed them to crush and grind tough leaves and other vegetation.

PHYLOGENETIC TREE

PERMIAN	252 mya	TRIASSIC	201 mya	JURASSIC	145 mya	CRETACEOUS	66 mya
						Hadrosaurs	
				Ornithopods			
Ornithischians						Iguanodonts	

SKELETON

Vertebrae

Skull

Tailbones

MALE CRESTS
Corythosaurus males would have had larger crests than the female dinosaurs.

FOOT STRUCTURE
Corythosaurus had three thick toes that did not have claws, but ended in wide hooves. This foot structure helped the dinosaur to walk on all types of land surfaces.

Corythosaurus

SKIN
The skin of *Corythosaurus* was covered by scales, spread evenly all over the body.

BEHAVIOR
When feeding, *Corythosaurus* might have joined other herbivorous dinosaurs. These dinosaurs lived in herds and possibly moved regularly from one area to another.

CREST SIZES
The crest sizes would have varied depending on the gender and on the age of the animal.

SHORT ARMS
The arms were shorter than the legs. The study of footprints of hadrosaurs indicates that they walked mainly on four legs.

Head Crests

In a Mesozoic world filled with predators and competitors, it was important for dinosaurs to be able to communicate with and recognize each other. It was also vital for them to be able to defend themselves.

Dinosaurs developed a variety of structures to help them recognize each other as members of the same species. Head crests were one of these features.

Herbivorous beaked dinosaurs, such as *Triceratops,* had the most developed head crests of all, with huge horns and massive neck plates (see pages 110–115). The birdlike dinosaurs, such as *Parasaurolophus,* had hollow crests that allowed them to make deep sounds. These structures helped to identify the members of a group, but were not strong enough to defend the animals in fights. Pachycephalosaurs, however, had dome-shaped, thickened heads, which they may have used to defend themselves.

Some carnivorous theropods also developed odd-looking skulls. Early dinosaurs, such as *Dilophosaurus,* had crests on their heads. Later on in the Jurassic period, both *Cryolophosaurus* and *Monolophosaurus* developed crests. We are still unsure today what these rather strange growths were used for.

In 2013, paleontologists discovered skin impressions of a soft structure resembling a rooster's wattle. These belonged to the hadrosaur *Edmontosaurus.*

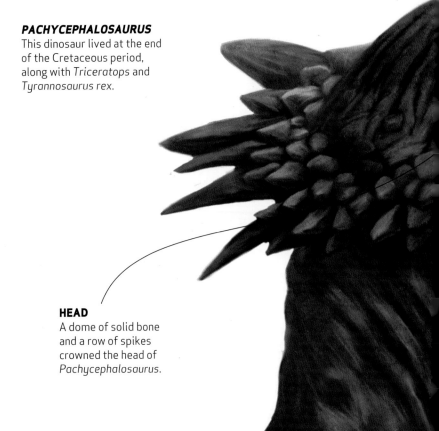

PACHYCEPHALOSAURUS
This dinosaur lived at the end of the Cretaceous period, along with *Triceratops* and *Tyrannosaurus rex.*

HEAD
A dome of solid bone and a row of spikes crowned the head of *Pachycephalosaurus.*

COLOR AND CAMOUFLAGE

Body color and patterns (camouflage) allow animals to blend in with their environment, making them difficult to spot. Scientists believe that dinosaurs developed camouflage and other adaptations according to the environment around them.

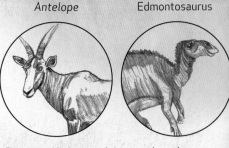

Antelope   Edmontosaurus

Dinosaurs living on plains may have been similar to antelopes in body color.

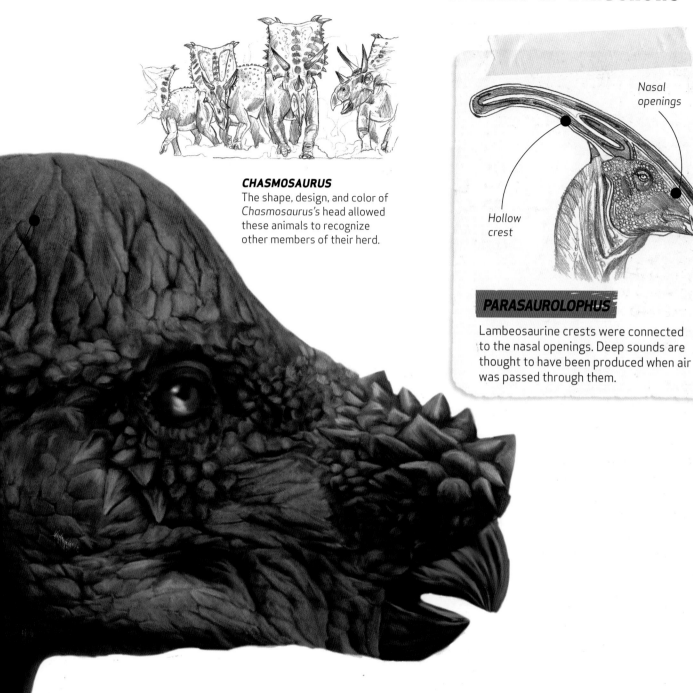

CHASMOSAURUS
The shape, design, and color of *Chasmosaurus's* head allowed these animals to recognize other members of their herd.

Nasal openings

Hollow crest

PARASAUROLOPHUS
Lambeosaurine crests were connected to the nasal openings. Deep sounds are thought to have been produced when air was passed through them.

Coelophysis could have possibly had stripes like a tiger, in order to hide among plants and trees.

Tiger

Coelophysis

Deer

Talenkauen

Some dinosaurs may have had light-colored spots, similar to deer, to match the dappled (spotty) light in woods.

Body Armor

Both the ankylosaurs and the stegosaurs developed bizarre body coverings for protection. These included spikes, plates, and shields. Stegosaurs had a double row of plates running along the body, with a bunch of spikes at the end of the tail, which they used to defend themselves against predators and competitors. Ankylosaurs were four-legged, with low, strong bodies. They protected themselves from attack by resting their soft bellies on the ground. The spikes and plates on their backs saved them from the bites and scratches of their attackers.

The herbivorous dinosaurs *Amargasaurus* and *Agustinia* both had more complex bony formations on their backs for protection.

AMARGASAURUS

The Argentinean paleontologist José Bonaparte found this herbivorous dinosaur of the Cretaceous period in Patagonia, Argentina, in 1991. From each of the vertebrae along its neck and back grew tall spines. Scientists are unsure what these spines were used for, but we know that they grew up to 30 inches in length along the dinosaur's neck. There were two rows of spines, which got smaller toward the back and became a single row near the hips.

AGUSTINIA

Agustinia had a double set of long plates on top of its neck, back, and tail. These plates helped to protect it from carnivores and were also used for recognition.

SPINES
Scientists have debated what these spines would have looked like in real life. They may have been covered in skin or horny growths. If more fossils are discovered in the future, then we may find out more information.

BACK
It's possible that *Amargasaurus* had a hump of fat along its raised back.

SPIKED NECK
When bending its neck downward, the animal showed its great fan of spikes.

HEAD
Amargasaurus had a small head and thin, cylindrical teeth.

PROTECTION AND RECOGNITION

The skulls of ankylosaurs were armor-plated and hardened, while some theropods had identifying crests.

Euoplocephalus and *Edmontonia* had hardened eyelids.

Cryolophosaurus had a fan-shaped crest.

Citipati had an unusually tall crest on top of its skull.

Pachycephalosaurus

Pachycephalosaur means "thick-headed reptile," and it is likely these dinosaurs used their tough heads to defend themselves.

Pachycephalosaurus may be one of the most extraordinary-looking dinosaurs, with its domed skull and cone-shaped growths. It was two-legged, with long, strong hind legs and short front limbs. Its hips were wide, indicating that it had a large stomach that was able to contain and digest lots of vegetation.

The narrow beak at the end of the mouth had teeth of different shapes. At the upper tip of the snout, the teeth were cone-shaped and good for biting, whereas the ones at the sides of the cheek were leaf-shaped with sawlike edges. It is thought that pachycephalosaurs used their heads as powerful weapons in a fight. Their necks were strong to withstand the impact of head-on collisions or sideswipes.

Pachycephalosaurs are closely related to the ceratopsians, so they are part of the Marginocephalia group. Dinosaurs in this group all have a skull with an outgrowth over the rear of the neck. In ceratopsians, this outgrowth consisted of delicate neck frills, but in pachycephalosaurs it was a series of cone-shaped knobs.

TAIL
Pachycephalosaurus had a very thick tail, with a mesh of tissues at the end to increase its strength.

GENUS: PACHYCEPHALOSAURUS
CLASSIFICATION: ORNITHISCHIA, MARGINOCEPHALIA, PACHYCEPHALOSAURIA

SPEEDY
With its long, powerful legs, *Pachycephalosaurus* could run at great speed.

LENGTH 15 ft
WEIGHT 1,000 lb
DIET Herbivorous

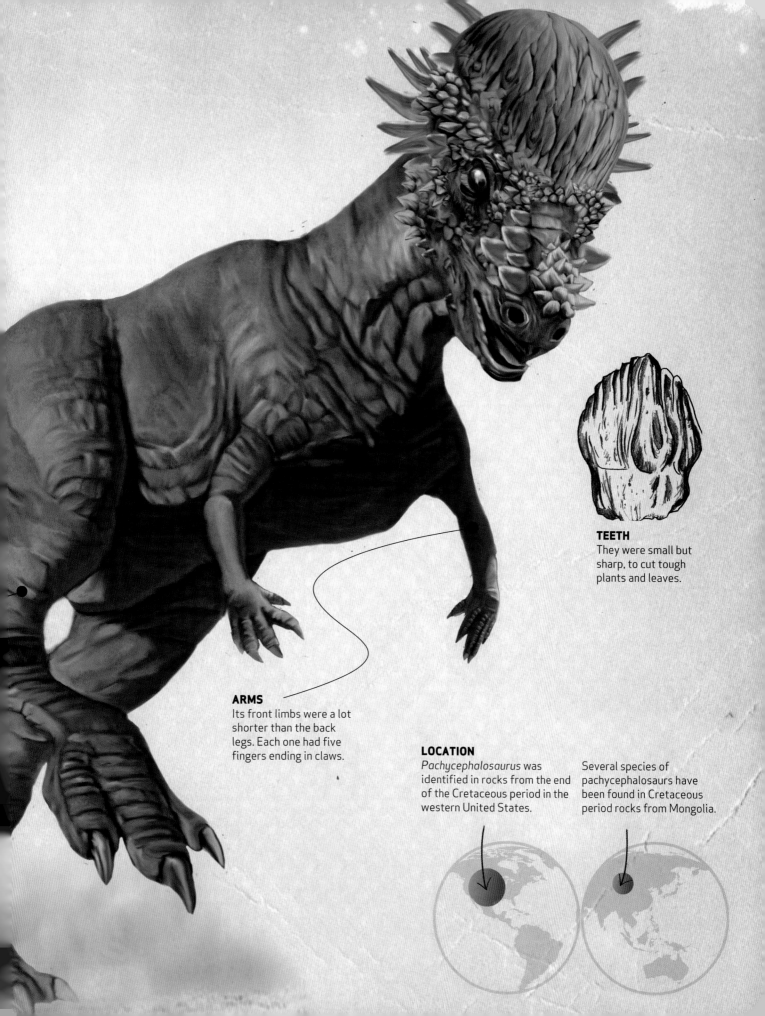

TEETH
They were small but sharp, to cut tough plants and leaves.

ARMS
Its front limbs were a lot shorter than the back legs. Each one had five fingers ending in claws.

LOCATION
Pachycephalosaurus was identified in rocks from the end of the Cretaceous period in the western United States.

Several species of pachycephalosaurs have been found in Cretaceous period rocks from Mongolia.

Pachycephalosaurus

During the last 20 million years of the Cretaceous period, dinosaurs of the Marginocephalia group evolved in North America and Asia. *Pachycephalosaurus* and *Stegoceras* appeared in the western United States, and *Homocephale* and *Prenocephale* in the Gobi Desert of Mongolia.

Pachycephalosaurus was the largest member of Marginocephalia, measuring almost 15 feet long. The dome of the skull increased in height as the animal grew, and in males it was taller and more curved than in females.

Pachycephalosaurus's eyes were set inside large, deep cavities, which protected them during fights. The muscles of the neck were very powerful, and the backbone was built to withstand impacts. Its wide hips helped the animal to keep its balance.

DIVERSITY OF PACHYCEPHALOSAURS

A large number of different skull types have been discovered in North America and Mongolia. Scientists debate whether these are all different species or whether they just represent different growth patterns in males and females. It was also announced in 2009 that two species of pachycephalosaurs were really just fossils of juveniles from other species.

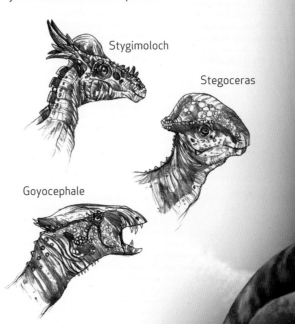

Stygimoloch

Stegoceras

Goyocephale

PHYLOGENETIC TREE

PERMIAN	252 mya	TRIASSIC	201 mya	JURASSIC	145 mya	CRETACEOUS	66 mya

Marginocephalians

Ornithischians

Pachycephalosaurs

Ceratopsians

SKULL
Pachycephalosaurus had a large skull with a dome about 10 inches in height, protecting a tiny brain!

Pachycephalosaurus

SKULL
The skull was attached to the spine and neck with very strong muscles and tendons. This added strength must have been important to *Pachycephalosaurus*, but scientists are still unsure exactly how.

HIPS
The hips were wide, which has led some scientists to believe that these dinosaurs fought each other from the side.

LEGS
The shape of the bones show they were able to run fast and crash against an enemy.

LONG BACKBONE
It had long been thought that *Pachycephalosaurus* held its body straight, so that the shock of head butting was absorbed along the whole length of the backbone. We know now that its neck was more of a U shape, so this theory may no longer be true.

Bird Evolution

Fossil history shows us the process of evolution that led to the development of birds from small feathered theropods, such as *Velociraptor*.

I t was the English naturalist Thomas Huxley who realized that the carnivorous *Compsognathus* and the oldest known bird, *Archaeopteryx*, shared the same type of back legs. This is how the theory that birds descended from dinosaurs was first developed.

The idea of a relationship between dinosaurs and birds was revived by paleontologist John Ostrom (see page 100), with his discovery of the theropod *Deinonychus*. He found some extraordinary similarities between *Deinonychus* and *Archaeopteryx*.

In recent years, more evidence has been found to support the dinosaur–bird relationship. In China, paleontologists discovered hundreds of rocks with complete specimens of *Caudipteryx* and *Microraptor*, which showed the presence of different types of feathers. In Mongolia, they found skeletons of *Oviraptors* sitting on their eggs. However, it is *Unenlagia* (half-bird) that is the most birdlike dinosaur found so far.

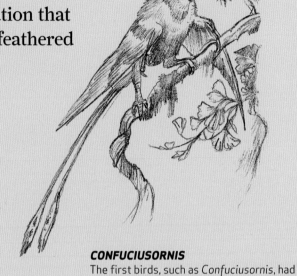

CONFUCIUSORNIS
The first birds, such as *Confuciusornis*, had teeth and were roughly the size of pigeons.

LONG STEPS
The femur (thigh bone) was adapted for running.

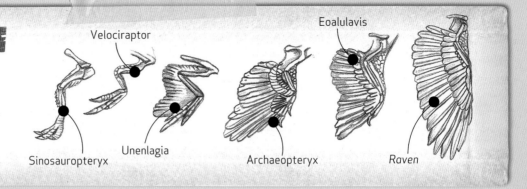

ARMS INTO WINGS

The lengthening of the arms and their feathers, together with the ability to flap with force, led to the appearance of wings.

Velociraptor

Eoalulavis

Sinosauropteryx

Unenlagia

Archaeopteryx

Raven

FEATHERED ARMS
Unenlagia was able to flap its arms, but it could not fly!

TEARING TEETH
Unenlagia's small teeth were useful for tearing, but not for chewing food.

ACTIVE HUNTERS
With the help of their large eyes and brains, avian (birdlike) theropods could judge the movement and distance of their prey.

SKELETON
Unenlagia's long arms show the stage from which the wings of ancient birds, such as *Archaeopteryx*, developed. The second toes of its feet had large, sickle-shaped claws, which were used for hunting and fighting.

THORAX
The furcula or "wishbone" was fused.

TAIL
The tail had 16 bones.

BONES
The bones were hollow to reduce weight.

ARMS
The first digit (finger) of the arms was shortened—a feature of wings.

Bird Evolution

The skeleton of *Unenlagia* was found in Cretaceous period rocks from Patagonia, Argentina. The fossil shows us that the arms of these advanced theropods moved in the same way as birds' wings. The body structure of *Unenlagia* indicates that this animal was at a development stage between theropods, such as *Deinonychus,* and ancient birds, such as *Archaeopteryx.*

Until quite recently, no Mesozoic fossils with feathers had been found since *Archaeopteryx,* in 1862. However, since the 1990s, a number of small dinosaurs with feathered bodies have been discovered in Liaoning, China. These fossils were preserved very well in soft mud in a lake from the Early Cretaceous period.

MICRORAPTOR

The majority of dinosaurs with feathers are included in the group Maniraptora. Small forms, such as *Dilong,* had well-developed feathers, but other big forms, such as *Tyrannosaurus,* did not have them. *Microraptor* was a bit less than 3 feet long and was a relative of *Deinonychus* and *Unenlagia.* It had four wings! Its front limbs and back legs had long, wide feathers that helped it to glide and fly. *Microraptor* threw itself from trees, then used its front wings to glide and possibly flap, and its back wings to control its motion—like a rudder. The contents of its stomach showed that it hunted tiny mammals.

EGG-SITTER
Birds got the habit of sitting on their nests to protect and provide warmth to their eggs from their theropod ancestors, such as *Oviraptor.*

FOSSILIZED BEHAVIOR

The fossilized skeleton of the small theropod *Mei long* (sleeping dragon) was found sitting on its heels, with its tail and neck around the body, and the snout under one arm. This position is similar to the one used by modern-day birds to keep warm and to rest.

Fossilized skeleton

Reconstruction

HIND FEATHERS
These feathers were used as a rudder to control the direction of flight.

CLUSTER OF FEATHERS
The pattern of feathers on the body of a dinosaur or bird is often preserved in fossils, too, showing where clumps of feathers grew or crests on the head were formed, for example.

FRONT WINGS
These were used for gliding and perhaps for flapping.

CLAWS
Microraptor clung to branches with its claws.

FEATHERED DINOSAURS
As a result of new discoveries, especially in China, there is now direct fossil evidence for feathers in at least 40 different species of dinosaurs. Due to this, scientists now agree that there is an evolutionary link between birds and dinosaurs.

Unenlagia

Caudipteryx

Caudipteryx had small winglike arms with claws. The feathers in its tail balanced the body and were used to identify it to other members of the same species.

C audipteryx (tail with feathers) was a species of *Oviraptor* about the same size as a present-day turkey. It was mainly a carnivorous dinosaur but it had omnivorous habits—it fed on both invertebrate animals and vegetation. Its head was small and high, with large eyes. It had a short snout with a horny beak and a few tiny, pointed teeth at the end. Some specimens of *Caudipteryx* have gastroliths (stomach stones) in the area of the gizzard, which indicates that it may also have eaten some seeds.

The fossils of this theropod show that the body was covered by short feathers which controlled its body temperature. Its arms were covered by longer feathers; however, these small wings were not fit for flying. The winglike arms and the feathers at the tip of the tail helped to balance the body when the animal was running, especially when it was turning.

GENUS: CAUDIPTERYX
CLASSIFICATION: SAURISCHIA, THEROPODA, MANIRAPTORA

SPEEDY RUNNER
The long legs, similar to those of a South American rhea, show that *Caudipteryx* was a fast runner.

LENGTH 3 ft
WEIGHT 7 lb
DIET Omnivorous

MOBILITY
The thin, flexible neck might have helped *Caudipteryx* to gather food.

DIET
With its narrow beak, *Caudipteryx* caught small invertebrates that were found in the bark of trees.

LOCATION
Maniraptor fossils have been found around the world. *Deinonychus* was discovered in the United States, and *Unenlagia* in Argentina.

Caudipteryx was found in Liaoning, China, along with fossils of other dinosaurs with feathers.

Caudipteryx

The maniraptors (seizing hands) are the theropod dinosaurs most closely related to birds. Their hands had three long fingers that ended in curved, pointed claws. The arms of these dinosaurs generally bent in a zigzag shape. They had a system of tissues and joints that made their hands automatically extend forward when stretching their arms. This feature is also shared by birds.

Among the most important maniraptors were oviraptors (such as *Caudipteryx*), therizinosaurs, and the alvarezsaurs (insect-eaters with tiny arms, such as *Alvarezsaurus*, *Patagonykus*, and *Mononykus*).

The main group of maniraptors was the deinonychosaurs. Their name (terrible or fearsome claw) refers to the large sickle-shaped claws on the second toes of their feet. These hunters ate all types of food, according to their body sizes: the tiny *Microraptor* hunted small mammals; *Velociraptor* preyed on bigger dinosaurs, such as *Protoceratops*; and *Austroraptor* hunted titanosaurs the size of present-day hippopotamuses.

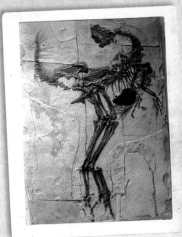

CHINESE SKELETONS
The dinosaur specimens from Liaoning, China, are preserved in rocks that are around 125 million years old. The rock layers where *Caudipteryx* was found also contained remains of other feathered dinosaurs, such as *Dilong* and *Sinornithosaurus*.

BIRDLIKE

The maniraptors include a large variety of birdlike theropods, with a variety of diets and a range of different levels of development in their arms.

Beipiaosaurus

Mononykus

Similicaudipteryx

PHYLOGENETIC TREE

PERMIAN	252 mya	TRIASSIC	201 mya	JURASSIC	145 mya	CRETACEOUS	66 mya
						Oviraptors	
				Coelurosaurs		Therizinosaurs	
			Tetanurans				
		Theropods					

COURTING
Caudipteryx may have displayed its colorful feathers with repetitive body movements to attract possible mates.

INCISIVOSAURUS
This cousin of *Caudipteryx* had large teeth at the tip of its snout, similar to those of rodents. The skull measured 4 inches.

Caudipteryx

NECK
The neck had a large number of bones, making movement easy.

SKELETON
The skeleton was adapted for swift movement.

HIND LEGS
Caudipteryx had long, slim legs. It could run quickly when chased by predators.

SKULL
It was small but tall. It had big eyes and a thin rough snout that was covered by a horny beak.

FEATHERED TAIL
The marks of the skin show that the feathers were arranged in a fan shape at the tip of the tail.

PREHISTORIC REPTILES

During the Mesozoic era, a wide variety of reptiles existed alongside the dinosaurs. Many of these reptiles reached gigantic sizes.

Life in the Depths

During the Mesozoic era, dinosaurs ruled the land. But in the seas and oceans, reptiles that were distantly related to dinosaurs dominated the marine ecosystem.

A variety of animals lived in the oceans during the Mesozoic era. Many groups of invertebrates appeared in Panthalassa, the ocean surrounding the supercontinent of Pangaea. They included jellyfish, corals, ammonites, oysters, sea urchins, sea lilies, and lobsters. Alongside these invertebrates were different types of fish and reptiles, such as ichthyosaurs (which looked like dolphins), plesiosaurs, mosasaurs, and different species of crocodiles. These reptiles formed part of a process of evolution that is often called the Mesozoic "marine revolution." This event began around 150 million years ago and gave rise to a large variety of animal life.

Even though certain reptiles had their origins on land, they adapted successfully to life underwater. This was possible due to changes in their bodies, including their lungs, that allowed them to move smoothly underwater. Plesiosaurs, for example, evolved flipper-like limbs to help them swim efficiently.

ARCHELON
Archelon was a huge sea turtle that appeared in the oceans around North America approximately 70 million years ago. It measured 13 feet in diameter! Theropod dinosaurs fed on its eggs, which it laid on beaches.

PREDATORS
Plesiosaurs were some of the largest predators in the oceans and lakes.

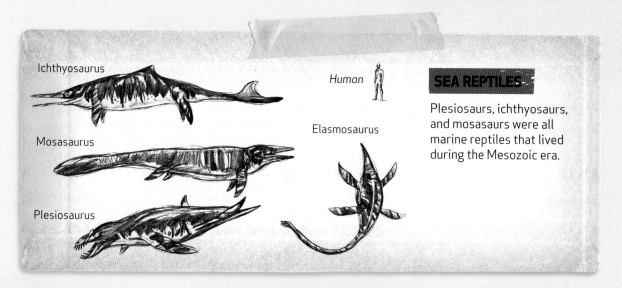

Ichthyosaurus

Human

Elasmosaurus

Mosasaurus

Plesiosaurus

SEA REPTILES

Plesiosaurs, ichthyosaurs, and mosasaurs were all marine reptiles that lived during the Mesozoic era.

ELASMOSAURUS

Elasmosaurus had an extremely long neck made up of more than 70 bones.

THE ORIGIN OF FLIPPERS

The plesiosaurs are included in the group Sauropterygia (lizard flippers). The oldest of this group did not have flippers, but their fingers were connected by a thin layer of skin that helped them to move in the water.

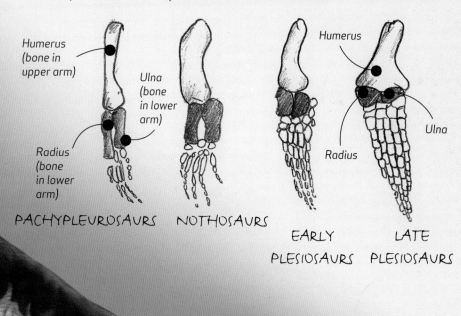

Humerus (bone in upper arm)

Ulna (bone in lower arm)

Radius (bone in lower arm)

Humerus

Ulna

Radius

PACHYPLEUROSAURS   NOTHOSAURS

EARLY PLESIOSAURS   LATE PLESIOSAURS

LONG NECK

Although it could twist its long neck back and forth, *Elasmosaurus* did not have the flexibility of modern-day tortoises or snakes.

Flying Lizards

Pterosaurs were the first vertebrate animals to fly. They inhabited a great variety of landscapes. But although pterosaurs appeared in many forms and adapted in an extraordinary way, they disappeared without leaving any descendants.

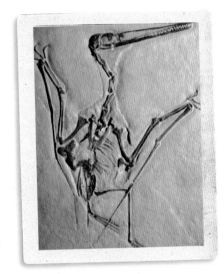

FRAGILE AND DELICATE
Pterosaurs had light, hollow bones, which made their fossilization difficult. There were very few early discoveries, so there is little detailed information from that time. However, now scientists have plenty of good fossils to study, so we are learning a lot more about these dinosaurs.

The name *pterosaur* means "winged lizard." They lived during the Mesozoic era, from around 225 million years ago to the end of the Cretaceous period, 66 million years ago. Pterosaurs were flying reptiles with forelimbs that were evolved into wings. The fourth finger was extremely long and supported an elastic skin structure (membrane) that was linked to the body.

Pterosaurs are close relatives of dinosaurs, but fossils of their ancestors are not known. It is thought that these ancestors must have been tree-dwelling reptiles with skin folds, which they used to help them glide.

In 1767, the first pterosaur remains were found in Germany. Since then, there have been many different theories about these animals—even the possibility that they were swimmers. But today, we know they were accomplished fliers.

Along with birds and bats, pterosaurs are the only flying vertebrate animals known. Powerful flying muscles were attached to their breastbones. The species that lived in more open spaces had long, narrow wings to help them glide. However, the ones living in woods or rocky areas had short, wide wings for more flexible movement.

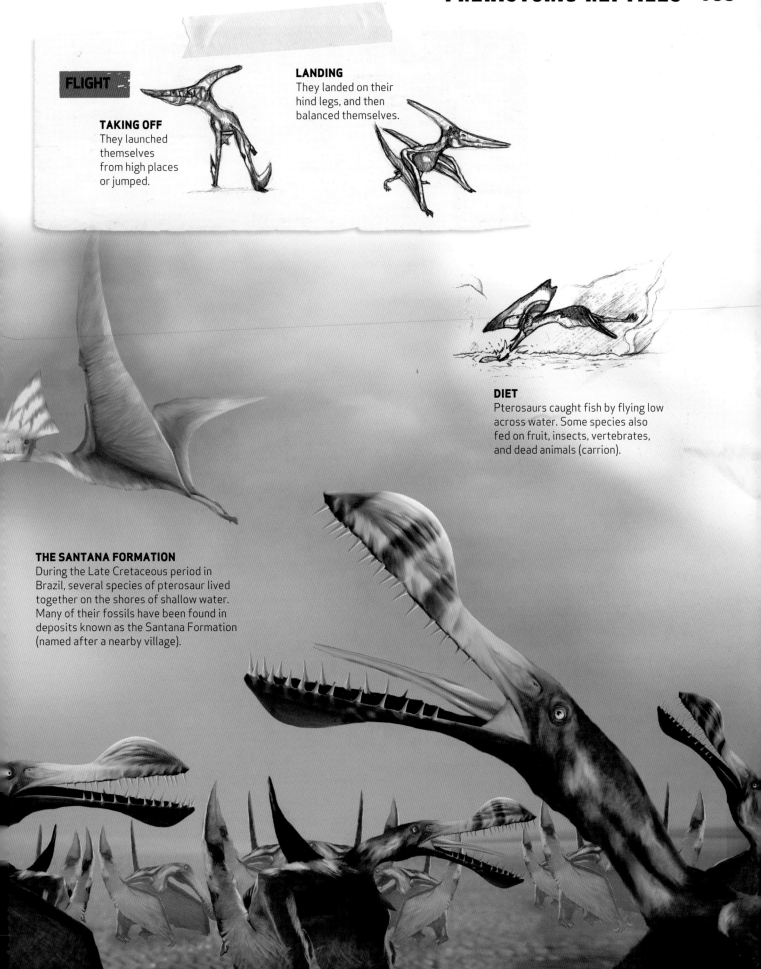

FLIGHT

TAKING OFF
They launched
themselves
from high places
or jumped.

LANDING
They landed on their
hind legs, and then
balanced themselves.

DIET
Pterosaurs caught fish by flying low
across water. Some species also
fed on fruit, insects, vertebrates,
and dead animals (carrion).

THE SANTANA FORMATION
During the Late Cretaceous period in
Brazil, several species of pterosaur lived
together on the shores of shallow water.
Many of their fossils have been found in
deposits known as the Santana Formation
(named after a nearby village).

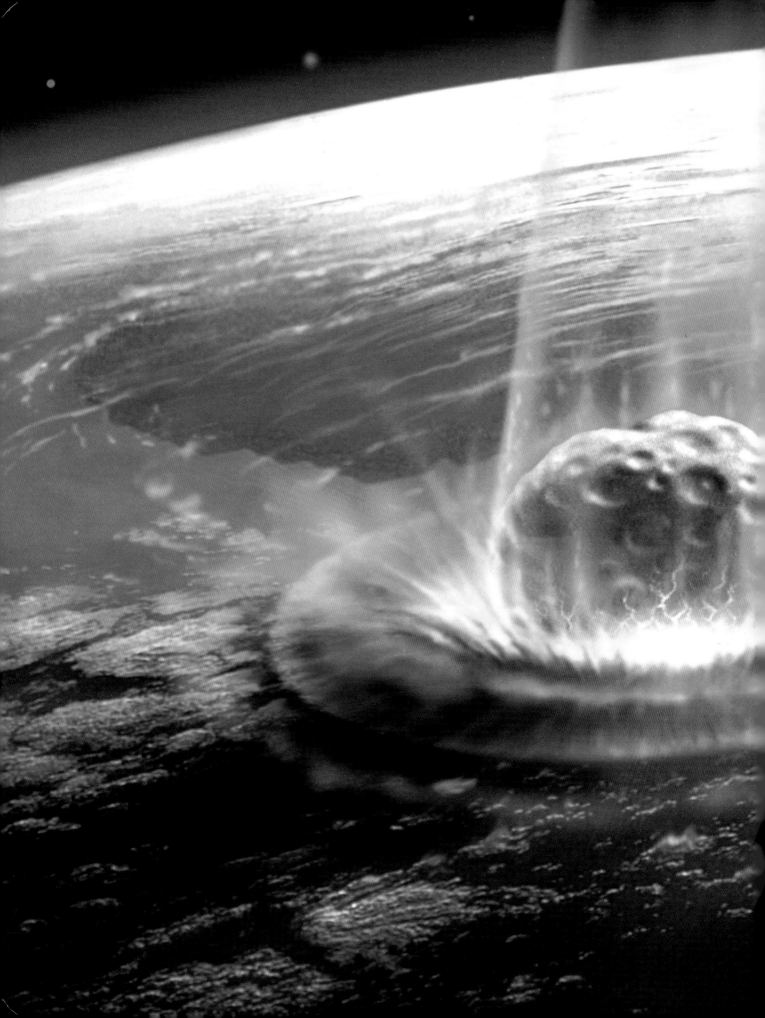

THE END OF AN ERA

Around 66 million years ago, the dinosaurs, along with a large number of other vertebrates, suddenly disappeared. There is much debate about what led to this mass extinction.

The Mystery of Extinction

Dinosaurs appeared in the Triassic period, taking the place of synapsids and other ancient reptiles. In the Jurassic period, they developed to huge sizes and, in the Cretaceous period, they were widespread and dominant—until they mysteriously disappeared.

The Mesozoic era started 252 million years ago, after a great extinction removed most of the synapsids from the Paleozoic era. During the Mesozoic, the most varied, common, and gigantic vertebrates were the reptiles. This group included marine animals, land animals, such as dinosaurs and crocodiles, and flying animals, including pterosaurs and birds.

The Mesozoic era finished 66 million years ago in the same way it had started—with a major extinction. The great disappearance at the end of the Cretaceous period left Earth with almost no large animals!

There are many theories to explain why this happened. One of the most popular is that Earth was struck by a large meteorite (a piece of rock from space). Although nothing has been proven, what we do know for certain is that a catastrophic event caused the disappearance of many species on land and in the ocean, bringing to an end the "golden age" of the reptiles.

LETHAL IMPACT

It is believed that a large meteorite struck Earth and its impact released large quantities of dust and vapor, which would have caused climate change on a global scale. Other theories suggest that a volcanic eruption may have caused a great release of gases and ash. The result would have been a drop in world temperatures and the formation of acid rain. In the long term, the dust and ash could have led to a greenhouse effect (a warming up of the layer of gases around Earth), which would have reduced the amount of sunlight reaching Earth and caused many animals and plants to die.

LAYER OF IRIDIUM
The unusual amount of this rare chemical element found in rocks dating from the end of the Cretaceous period supports the idea of a meteorite hitting Earth.

BEE FOSSIL
Many groups of animals, including insects, managed to survive the destruction.

THE CHICXULUB CRATER

A crater in the Yucatán Peninsula, Mexico, was produced by a meteorite of around 6 miles in diameter that hit Earth at the end of the Cretaceous period. Scientists believe this impact may have caused the extinction of the dinosaurs.

Mexico

Gulf of Mexico

Yucatán

Index